MUSIC AND MUSICIANS

AN INTRODUCTION

Stephen Valdez
Study Guide
TO ACCOMPANY

MUSIC AND MUSICIANS

AN INTRODUCTION

DONALD D. MEGILL
Mira Costa College

Prentice Hall, Englewood Cliffs, New Jersey 07632

Acquisitions editor: *Norwell Therien, Jr.*
Supplements acquisitions editor: *Marion R. Gottlieb*
Editorial/production supervision: *Robert C. Walters*
Production coordinator: *Robert M. Anderson*

© 1994 by Prentice-Hall, Inc.
A Paramount Communications Company
Englewood Cliffs, New Jersey 07632

Printed in the United States of America

10   9   8   7   6   5   4   3   2   1

ISBN   0-13-605817-5

PRENTICE-HALL INTERNATIONAL (UK) LIMITED, LONDON
PRENTICE-HALL OF AUSTRALIA PTY. LIMITED, SYDNEY
PRENTICE-HALL CANADA INC. TORONTO
PRENTICE-HALL HISPANOAMERICANA, S.A., MEXICO
PRENTICE-HALL OF INDIA PRIVATE LIMITED, NEW DELHI
PRENTICE-HALL OF JAPAN, INC., TOKYO
SIMON & SCHUSTER ASIA PTE. LTD., SINGAPORE
EDITORA PRENTICE-HALL DO BRASIL, LTDA., RIO DE JANEIRO

Table of Contents

PREFACE

This study guide is designed to accompany <u>Music & Musicians</u> by Donald D. Megill. The study guide is organized in the same way as the textbook so that the student can easily adapt the study guide to the format of the book. The first four chapters discuss the fundamental elements of music. These are followed by eight chapters that discuss the music of the various periods of music history, from the medieval period to the present. The chapters are followed in turn by ten Topics chapters which discuss specific genres of music or specific aspects of music production.

Each chapter of the study guide is laid out in the following manner:

1. An outline of the information discussed by Prof. Megill. In most cases, the wording is almost exactly the same material as Megill has written, but in a concise outline format. In a few instances, the exact wording has been altered for the sake of space, but the ideas presented by Prof. Megill have not been altered in any way. These are his words and his ideas in an easy to-study outline form.

2. The outline is followed by a set of exercises designed for the student to experiment with other musical examples and, in some cases, to experiment with ways to make music on your own. Most of the exercises require the student to listen to recordings by the composers discussed in the chapters. However, these are examples that are not discussed in the text. Rather they are examples that will help the student to further understand a specific form or compositional technique or style of music. Most, if not all, of the recordings recommended for these exercises should be available at your school library. All the exercises require a written record of the student's experiences with the music suggested. But most of all, the exercises have been designed for the student to have fun with the examples suggested. Please feel free to adapt the exercises for your specific needs.

3. The exercises are followed by several study questions to help the student prepare for exams. The questions were formulated from the text itself and in many cases the wording of a question is almost exactly as it appears in the text. This was done specifically to help the student find the information as it is discussed in the text. The questions are in various formats--multiple choice, true and false, fill in the blank, and short answer.

It is my sincere wish that this study guide help in your music studies. Use it to supplement the textbook, not substitute for it. Use it to help you enjoy and understand the music that you hear. It is a wonderful and exciting field of study that is good for the soul.

I would like to thank Kathy Shawhan and Bud Therien at Prentice Hall for giving me the opportunity to prepare this study guide. I would also like to acknowledge Donald Megill, without whose book there would be no need for this study guide. And finally, I would like to thank my wife Cherese for her editing and proof-reading of this manuscript.

Stephen Valdez
University of Oregon
Eugene, Oregon

CHAPTER 1, SOUND: The Foundation of Music

This chapter deals with the physical properties of sound, the function of sound and the sources of sound. The laws of physics determine the resulting sound when two or more different notes are combined, but taste and style determine whether the combined sounds are pleasing to the ear or create tension. If a sound is pleasing, we say that it is CONSONANT; if the sound creates any amount of tension, we say that it is DISSONANT.

Physics also tells us that any pitch produced by any sound source includes not only the principal or FUNDAMENTAL PITCH, but is also flavored with many different, softer-sounding tones that are produced simultaneously with the fundamental pitch. These notes are collectively known as the OVERTONE SERIES.

I. Sound Waves (pp. 18-20)

    A. Properties of Sound Waves

        1. Move in waves as air molecules bump into each other

        2. The eardrum perceives movement of air molecules

        3. Pitch determined by speed of the waves

        4. Sound waves have many shapes depending on the audible overtones above the fundamental pitch

    B. Qualities of Sound Wave Shapes

        1. Height and depth of a wave determines the AMPLITUDE or volume of a tone

        2. Length of a wave determines the FREQUENCY or pitch of a tone

            a. Frequency is equal to the number of vibrations per second that occur in a given pitch

            b. Every pitch has a specific frequency

            c. Lower notes have longer waves and vice versa

        3. Synthesizers

            a. Electronic tone generators

            b. Can imitate acoustic sound waves

            c. Can invent new sounds by changing wave shapes

    C. Intonation

        1. Accuracy of pitch, being "in tune"

        2. Matching the pitch of one instrument against another

        3. Bringing two or more instruments into agreement on a given pitch; TUNING UP

        4. Instruments in an orchestra typically tune to the pitch A 440, which vibrates 440 times per second

5. Playing out of tune can create dissonance

II. Sources of Sound (p. 20)

    A. The most common sounds occur in nature

    B. Traditional sounds in music are based on familiarity

    C. Contemporary composers use all kinds of sounds

        1. Natural sounds

        2. Instrumental sounds

        3. Mechanical sounds

    D. Any sound used in musical composition is "musical"

    E. The synthesizer is the most recent instrument available for composers

        1. Can create (generate) newly invented sounds by manipulating wave forms

        2. Can recreate traditional sounds by imitating existing wave forms (SAMPLING)

            a. Wave forms of acoustic instruments are analyzed

            b. Sampled waves are rebuilt to match acoustic waves

            c. Sampled sounds are stored on a synthesizer computer

EXERCISES

1. Compare one of the sets of instruments listed below. Inspect the instruments closely to see how they are made, the material from which they are made, and how they produce sound. Write a brief essay on your findings.

    a. Acoustic guitar and violin (or viola or cello)   b.   Clarinet and oboe

    c. Clarinet and flute   d.   Trumpet and horn (or trombone)

2. Get together with two to five classmates and create a short musical composition that uses the following sounds:

    a. Traditional musical instruments

    b. Mechanical sounds* (running motors, traffic sounds, etc.)

    c. Natural sounds* (dogs barking, birds, river flowing, etc.)

        (*Record on tape for class presentations)

3. Using a two-foot length of wood (2" by 4"), two nails or wood screws (one at each end of the board), and a length of wire (clothesline wire, speaker wire, or a used guitar string), make a MONOCHORD. Stretch the wire as tight as you can between the nails. Experiment with the one-string instrument by plucking the string with different objects (your finger, a stick, a guitar pick). Using a small wedge of wood placed under the wire to change the length of the vibrations, observe the changes as you

lengthen or shorten the vibrating wire. Can you relate this to the discussion of the fundamental sound and the overtone series? Write up your observations in a brief report.

STUDY QUESTIONS

1. Two notes which are played together and sound pleasing to the listener are said to be (p. 17)

   A.   Consequent

   B.   Antecedent

   C.   Consonant

   D.   Dissonant

2. All pitches consist of several other tones that sound simultaneously, called the
   ___Overtone___ ___series___. (p. 17)

3. The fundamental pitch is the note that is hardest to hear. (p. 17)

   A.   True

   B.   False

4. A combination of tones that sound harsh or tense is called (p. 17)

   A.   Consequent

   B.   Antecedent

   C.   Consonant

   D.   Dissonant

5. An electronic tone generator that imitates acoustic instruments is called (p. 18)

   A.   A keyboard

   B.   A synthesizer

   C.   An amplifier

   D.   A quasi-conductor

6. The volume of a sound is called frequency. (p. 18)

   A.   True

   B.   False

7. The number of vibrations per second in a specific pitch is called (p. 18)

   A.   Intonation

   B.   Amplitude

   C.   Consonance

   D.   Frequency

8. Exact matching of a specific pitch by several instruments will produce good
   ___Intonation___. (p. 18)

9. The re-creation of natural wave forms on a synthesizer is called ___sampling___ (p. 20)

3

10. Traditional sounds in music are based on familiarity with these sounds. (p. 20)

    A. True

    B. False

11. Using motors and other machine sounds in music resulted in a style called
    _____industrial_____ music. (p. 20)

CHAPTER 2, MUSICAL INSTRUMENTS: Traditional and Nontraditional

This chapter is concerned with the various instruments that are used to make music in the Western European/American culture. The author discusses the standard instruments used in orchestral music-- strings, woodwinds, brass, and percussion--as being TRADITIONAL INSTRUMENTS. There is also a discussion of instruments that are typically used in jazz and rock ensembles, which the author terms NONTRADITIONAL INSTRUMENTS. Also included in the nontraditional category is the electronic Musical Instrument Digital Interface, or MIDI.

In discussing the traditional instruments, the author also addresses the development of the orchestra. As new instruments were invented and developed, more of these instruments were accepted into the standard orchestra. New instruments were necessary to add contrasting timbres and to blend with the established instruments of the orchestra.

I. The Four Instrumental Families (pp. 22-25)

   A. Stringed Instruments (pp. 22-23)

      1. Have strings of varied lengths and widths

      2. String is made to vibrate by the performer

         a. Drawing a BOW across the strings

         b. PLUCKING the strings

      3. String length determines the instrument's range

         a. Longer string, lower pitch

         b. Performer's fingers press string to finger board, change the string length

         c. Smaller instruments have shorter strings, play higher than larger instruments

      4. Most common bowed string instruments today

         a. VIOLIN

         b. VIOLA

         c. CELLO

         d. BASS

      5. These instruments can also be plucked--PIZZICATO

      6. String instruments that are plucked or strummed include

         a. GUITAR

         b. LUTE

         c. MANDOLIN

         d. BANJO

         e. HARP

7. Plucking and strumming results in a percussive, rhythmic sound

B. Woodwinds (pp. 23-24)

    1. Name "woodwinds" comes from the fact that early wind instruments were made of wood

    2. Air is blown through instrument to activate vibrations

    3. Different types of instruments

        a. Non-reed instruments

           i. FLUTE

           ii. RECORDER

        b. Single-reed instruments

           i. CLARINET

           ii. SAXOPHONE

        c. Double-reed instruments

           i. OBOE

           ii. ENGLISH HORN

           iii. BASSOON

    4. Woodwinds have several keys that cover holes in the body of the instrument

        a. When holes are closed, air goes further into the body of the instrument

        b. This lowers the pitch of the instrument because the vibrating air column in the instrument is lengthened

C. Brass instruments (pp. 24-25)

    1. Long, tubular, metal instruments

    2. The performer's buzzing lips in a metal mouthpiece create a tone

        a. Pitch changes made by buzzing lips faster or slower

        b. Many notes can be played without changing the length of the instrument

        c. Faster buzzes can create different tones of the overtone series

    3. Valves are used to change pitch

        a. Developed in the early 19th century

        b. Depressing valve opens more tubing, changes the length of the instrument

        c. Performer can play notes outside the overtone series

        d. Trombone's slide changes that instrument's length

    4. Varied lengths and BORES (widths) of tubing creates low and high instruments

        a. Small, high instruments

           i. TRUMPET

           ii. FLUGEL HORN

           iii. FRENCH HORN

        b. Large, low instruments

        i.   TROMBONE

        ii.   BARITONE

        iii.   TUBA

D. Percussion instruments (p. 25)

    1.   Any struck sound source is a percussion instrument

    2.   DRUMS have a skin or membrane stretched over the body of the instrument

    3.   Various materials are used in making percussion instruments

        a. Wood

            i.   WOOD BLOCKS

            ii.   SHAKERS (MARACAS)

        b. Metal

            i.   CYMBALS

            ii.   BELLS

            iii.   TRIANGLES

            iv.   GONGS

    4.   Pitched percussion

        a.   CHIMES

        b.   GLOCKENSPIEL

        c.   XYLOPHONE

        d.   VIBRAPHONE

        e.   MARIMBA

        f.   TUBULAR BELLS

    5.   Hybrid percussion/string instruments

        a.   PIANO

        b.   HARPSICHORD

        c.   HARP

II. Instrumental Ensembles (pp. 25-29)

A. Instruments from the same family blend with each other

    1.   Often grouped in small ensembles of high and low instruments (e.g., STRING QUARTET)

B. Large ensembles use instruments from each family (e.g., the ORCHESTRA)

    1.   Like instruments blend with each other

    2.   Different instruments contrast with each other

C. Composers usually favored popular instruments of their own time

    1.   As certain instruments faded from favor, composers focused on more currently popular instruments

    2.   Music from different historical periods can often be identified by the instrument used

D. Instruments in the Early Orchestra (1600-1700; p. 27)

    1. Early bowed string instruments (VIOLS) replaced by members of the violin family

    2. Lute was replaced by the guitar

    3. Recorders, oboes, and bassoons were the principal wind instruments

    4. Foundation of harmony and rhythm was supplied by the harpsichord

    5. Other instruments used (for military, march sound)

        a. Valveless trumpet

        b. Valveless horn

        c. Kettledrums (TIMPANI)

        d. Bass drum

        e. Side drum

E. Instruments new to the Modern Orchestra (since 1700; p. 27)

    1. Performance techniques and instrumental design developed rapidly

    2. Sections expanded in size

        a. Flutes replaced recorders by 1750

        b. Paired woodwinds by 1780--two flutes, two oboes, two clarinets, two bassoons

        c. Early 19th century orchestras included two trumpets, four French horns, three trombones, and one tuba

        d. Late 19th century orchestras added alto and bass flutes, bass clarinet, and contra bassoon to woodwind section

        e. Percussion section grew dramatically in the 19th century

        f. Keyboard instruments used in the orchestra only as solo instruments; harpsichord disappeared in the mid-18th century

        g. String family grew in size to the largest section

F. Instruments in Jazz (p. 29)

    1. Orchestra instruments used in popular music in the early 20th century

        a. Wind instruments favored as melodic instruments

        b. Clarinet, trumpet, trombone used in early Dixieland jazz

        c. Saxophone became the dominant instrument in jazz

    2. Jazz rhythm section

        a. Grew from banjo and tuba or solo piano to include guitar, string bass, and drums

        b. Guitar replaced banjo; string bass replaced tuba

    3. Recent additions include synthesizers that are controlled by keyboards, guitars, and wind instruments

    4. Large jazz bands in the 1920s grouped instruments into four sections

        a. REEDS--five saxophones; double on flute, clarinet

b. BRASS--four-five trumpets; some double on flugel horn

c. LOW BRASS--four-five trombones

d. RHYTHM--piano, guitar, string bass, drums

G. Instruments in Rock and Commercial Music (p. 29)

1. Instruments associated with folk music (e.g., the guitar) have become the principal instruments of rock and commercial music

2. Amplification gives the styles a distinctive sound

3. Rock and commercial music ensembles are essentially rhythm sections without wind or string sections

4. Typical ensemble consists of

a. Electric guitar(s)

b. Electric bass guitar

c. Keyboards (pianos, organs, and/or synthesizers)

d. Large drum set

e. Auxiliary percussion drawn mostly from Latin America

5. Film music uses various ensembles from modified string orchestra to rock bands, sometimes a single performer with several synthesizers

III. MIDI (Musical Instrument Digital Interface; pp. 30-31)

A. Sounds of acoustic instruments can be electronically reproduced by synthesizers (SAMPLING)

1. Sampled sounds can be controlled by one keyboard

2. Synthesizers, drum machines, etc. are linked together with computers

a. Computer can add studio sounds (e.g., ECHO, DELAY)

b. Computer stores sound and can reproduce sound on command and at any speed

B. All musical selections and decisions made by the composer are coordinated (SEQUENCED) for performance

1. All parts played separately and later combined

2. All parts played by one performer

3. Composer has complete control over the music

4. Becoming common practice in studio recordings and film soundtracks

IV. New Concepts in Instruments (p. 31)

A. Musicians continue to experiment in developing instruments

B. Ideas of new sounds or sound combinations influence musicians

C. Composers and performers keep looking for technical improvements to expand capabilities of instruments

D. The "ideal sound" changes from one style period to the next

9

E. Any sound in music composition must be able to be controlled in order to reproduce that sound on request

F. The possibilities of new sounds are endless

EXERCISES

1. Listen to two of the following pieces of music and write a brief paper describing what you hear. What instruments are presented? How does the composer use various instruments to describe a feeling or an event in the music? Did you like these pieces? Why or why not?

A. Benjamin Britten: *A Young Person's Guide to the Orchestra*

B. Sergei Prokofiev: *Peter and the Wolf*

C. Camille Saint-Saëns: *Carnival of the Animals*

2. Choose one symphonic work from each of the following groups. Listen to the first movements of your choices (the Strauss piece is a single-movement work) and look for the score of each piece in the library to find out what instruments the composers used for each work. Compare the three works in relation to the size of the orchestras, how the instrument families are used for blend and for contrast, if the composer uses all instruments at the same time, and so on. Write up your findings in a brief, one-page report.

GROUP 1	GROUP 2	GROUP 3
Haydn, Symphony No. 45	Beethoven, Symphony No. 3	Mahler, Symphony 8
Haydn, Symphony No. 88	Mendelssohn, Symphony No. 4	Strauss, *Don Juan*
Mozart, Symphony No. 29	Schubert, Symphony No. 8	Bruckner, Symphony 7

STUDY QUESTIONS

1. Music in the Western European tradition is written for instruments that are from the four groups __Strings__, __woods__, __Brass__ and __Percussion__. (p. 21)

2. Changes in instruments can be seen by looking at the changes in (p. 21)

A. The orchestra

B. Political leadership

C. Aesthetic philosophy

D. Church music

10

3. Instrument families share a common means of creating sound. (p. 21)

    A. True

    B. False

4. Large instruments produce ___low or long___ frequencies. (p. 22)

5. Sound is produced in the typical orchestral string instruments by (p. 22)

    Drawing a bow across the Strings

6. The technique of plucking the strings on a violin is called (p. 22)

    A. Pianissimo

    B. Prestissimo

    C. Pizzicato

    D. Prestidigitation

7. Which of the following pairs are NOT bowed instruments? (p. 22)

    A. Violin and Lute

    B. Guitar and Mandolin

    C. Cello and String bass

    D. Viola and Harp

8. Strumming a stringed instrument can produce a rhythmic or ___Percossive___ sound. (p. 23)

9. To create a sound in a woodwind instrument the player must (p. 23)

    A. Blow air through it

    B. Buzz the lips in the mouthpiece

    C. Swing it rapidly around one's head

    D. Cover the holes in the instrument's body

10. Clarinets and saxophones are ___Single___ reed instruments. (p. 23)

11. Bassoons and English horns are ___Double___ reed instruments. (p. 23)

12. To create a lower sound in woodwinds the player must uncover the finger holes. (p. 23)

    A. True

    B. False

13. Tones are produced in brass instruments by (p. 24)

    A. Blowing air through them

    B. Buzzing the lips in the mouthpiece

    C. Pushing the valves up and down

    D. Covering the holes in the instrument's body

14. Early brass instruments used keys or valves to change pitches. (p. 24)

    A. True

    B. False

15. Depressing a valve changes the length of the instrument by (p. 24)

    opening more tubing

16. On the trombone the _slide_ changes the length of the instrument. (p. 24)

17. The larger lengths and bores of brass instruments enable the instruments to play much higher sounds than smaller-bore instruments. (p. 24)

    A.   True

    B.   False

18. Any sound source that is _struck or hit_ is a percussion instrument. (p. 25)

19. The piano can also be considered a percussion instrument. (p. 25)

    A.   True

    B.   False

20. Which of the following percussion instruments are made of metal? (p. 25)

    A.   Snare drums and Tympani

    B.   Tympani and Cymbals

    C.   Woodblocks and Xylophones

    D.   Cymbals and Gongs

21. Instruments from the same family are often grouped together in ensembles because (p. 25)

    Because they blend well together

22. Large ensembles like orchestras use several instrument families to create (p. 27)

    A.   Consonance

    B.   Contrast

    C.   Contortion

    D.   Consequence

23. Music from different historical periods can be identified by the use of particular instruments. (p. 27)

    A.   True

    B.   False

24. The bowed string instrument that was the predecessor to the violin family was the _viol_ of the 17th century. (p. 27)

25. The predecessor of the piano was the _Harpsichord_. (p. 27)

26. One way in which the orchestra was enlarged after 1750 was to include _pairs_ of woodwind instruments. (p. 27)

27. After 1750 keyboard instruments typically appear in orchestras as (p. 27)

    A.   The harmonic foundation

    B.   The rhythmic foundation

    C.   Solo instruments

    D.   Percussion instruments

12

28. The first wind instruments to appear in Dixieland jazz were the _Clarinet_,
    the _trumpet_, and the _trombone_. (p. 29)

29. The woodwind instrument that plays a dominant role in jazz and popular music is the (p. 29)

    A. Flute

    B. Saxophone

    C. Clarinet

    D. Oboe

30. The only string family member to maintain a role of importance throughout jazz history is the (p. 29)

    A. Guitar

    B. Banjo

    C. Fiddle

    D. String bass

31. The rhythm section in large dance bands after 1920 typically consists of _Piano_,
    guitar, _bass_, and _drums_. (p. 29)

32. The most distinctive sound aspect of rock and commercial music is the use of (p. 29)

    A. Fast tempos

    B. Slow tempos

    C. Amplification

    D. Solo performers

33. The typical rock or commercial ensemble is an enlarged rhythm section. (p. 29)

    A. True

    B. False

34. The acronym MIDI stands for _musical instrument digital interface_. (p. 30)

35. Playing separate instrumental parts and storing them on computer files for later use is
    called _Sequencing_. (p. 30)

36. Composers who use MIDI techniques feel that they no longer have control over the
    creation of a piece of music. (p. 31)

    A. True

    B. False

37. Any sound to be used in a musical composition must be able to be controlled on request. (p. 31)

    A. True

    B. False

38. The "ideal sound" stays the same from one period to the next. (p. 31)

    A. True

    B. False

13

CHAPTER 3, FLEXIBLE MUSICAL ELEMENTS

Chapter 3 discusses the many musical elements that composers and performers use to create a musical work. These are the materials that a composer uses to fill MUSICAL SPACE, much like a painter might use different colors, shapes, and brush strokes on the canvas. The basic elements discussed in this chapter are MOTION, PITCH, TONE, HARMONY, and TEXTURE. In addition, the author discusses NOTATION, TONALITY and the importance of TONIC and DOMINANT HARMONY, and the move from tonality to ATONALITY.

I. Motion (p. 33)

    A. A continuous pulse in music is defined as motion

        1. RHYTHM is measured by an audible or implied PULSE

        2. Pulse is often referred to as the BEAT

        3. Different note values can serve as the beat

        4. The beat is whatever note value the composer chooses to count as the pulse

    B. Beats are organized into larger units

        1. Grouping pulses in even, predictable sounds results in METER

        2. An ACCENT on the first beat in a group helps define the metric pattern

        3. Groups of rhythmic units are called MEASURES

        4. Measures (or BARS) are separated in notation by BAR (or MEASURE) LINES

        5. Measured music is needed to identify rhythmic styles, such as dance meters

    C. Meter is represented in notation by the TIME (or METER) SIGNATURE

        1. Signature appears at the beginning of the printed musical line

        2. Top number indicates the number of beats per measure

        3. Bottom number indicates what note value is a beat

II. Pitch (pp. 34-36)

    A. Pitch is an important element to both melody and harmony

    B. Defines the RANGE of possible notes for each instrument

        1. Range determines each instrument's place in a large ensemble

        2. Each instrument has a specific range

        3. Different ranges have different tone qualities

    C. Every note has an ENVELOPE that consists of four parts

        1. ATTACK as the note begins

        2. DECAY as the sound dies out after the attack

        3. SUSTAIN at a volume level of the performer's choosing

        4. RELEASE as the performer stops the note

5. Each instrument's envelope is unique to that instrument

D. A logical progression of pitches is called MELODY

 1. Some melodies have very TUNEFUL qualities

 2. Other melodies are angular and difficult to sing

 3. Some melody notes move small distances (CONJUNCT)

 4. Some melody notes move wide distances (DISJUNCT)

E. Melodies can be shaped with ARTICULATION MARKINGS

 1. Marks placed above or below notes in the printed music

 2. Tell the performer to add EMPHASIS or EXPRESSION

 3. There are many symbols used to indicate articulation (see p. 36)

III. Tone (pp. 36-37)

A. Each instrument has a unique sound quality and is capable of various tone qualities

B. The tone of a single instrument can be modified by adding its sound to a second instrument

C. The possibilities of tone manipulation are infinite

 1. Combining tone colors is called ORCHESTRATION

 2. Sound and tone color can be adjusted by adding or subtracting instruments from the ensemble

 3. Orchestration also affects HARMONY and TEXTURE

D. The composer shares the control of musical elements with the conductor and the performer

E. The conductor and the performer can control TEMPO (speed) and DYNAMICS (volume)

 1. Changes in tempo and dynamics can alter the character of the music

 2. Tempo

 a. Faster tempos can increase the intensity

 b. Tempos are often stated in terms that allow some variation in interpretation (ALLEGRO, GRAVE)

 c. Composers from the 19th century on indicate the number of beats played each minute (METRONOME MARKING)

 d. A list of common tempos is given on page 37

 3. Dynamics

 a. Louder volumes can increase the intensity

 b. Changes in dynamics can add drama to the music

 c. Dynamics are indicated with symbols

 d. Dynamic range is from PIANISSIMO (very soft; *pp*) to FORTISSIMO (very loud; *ff*)

 e. Dynamic levels are relative to each other

 4. Performers make musical decisions by interpreting dynamic and style markings

IV. Harmony (p. 38)

    A. The simultaneous combination of three or more different pitches is called a CHORD

        1. Many different chords in a piece of music

        2. Each chord has a relationship to other chords

        3. Chords made of notes that blend well are CONSONANT

        4. Chords that are full of tension are DISSONANT

    B. The way in which chords move and are perceived in relation to each other determines the harmony

        1. Harmony helps create moods and textures

        2. HARMONIC RHYTHM may indicate a regular chord pattern

        3. Chords may reinforce meter

        4. Chords may shape PHRASES

V. Texture (pp. 38-39)

    A. Texture results from the interaction of pitch, harmony, and motion

        1. Increased intensity in various musical elements thickens the overall texture

        2. Change in pitch and dynamic ranges can affect texture

        3. Texture fluctuates with each combination and change in range and activity

    B. There are three identifiable textures that coincide with the development of music since c. 900 A.D.

        1. MONOPHONY

            a. A single melodic idea

            b. Has no type of accompaniment

            c. Used in early church chant (GREGORIAN CHANT)

        2. POLYPHONY (COUNTERPOINT)

            a. Two or more INDEPENDENT, simultaneous melodies

            b. Each melody is equally important

            c. Each melody has its own character yet can still support the other melodies

        3. HOMOPHONY

            a. A single melody over subordinate parts

            b. Underlying parts provide chordal accompaniment

    C. Composers often combine these three textures in one piece to create an interesting variety of texture

VI. Symbols: Traditional and Nontraditional Notation (pp. 39-42)

    A. Musical notation has changed from that of early music to contemporary compositions

        1. Symbols change as new sounds are discovered

        2. Notation has developed from the early practices of the oral transmission of music

16

3. Notation was developed to help organize larger groups of performers

4. Some modern notation is very explicit in order for performers to interpret the composer's exact ideas

B. Elements of notation

1. The STAFF

    a. Device consisting of lines and spaces

    b. Defines exact pitches for musicians

    c. Places the pitches according to the musical alphabet

2. INTERVALS

    a. The distance between any two notes

    b. Intervals are described by HALF STEPS

        i. Large intervals have many half steps

        ii. Small intervals have fewer half steps

    c. Pitches on the staff may be altered higher or lower by half steps

        i. A SHARP alters a pitch a half step higher

        ii. A FLAT alters a pitch a half step lower

        iii. These alterations are called ACCIDENTALS

3. The piano KEYBOARD can be a visual aid for finding half steps

4. The OCTAVE

    a. The interval between two notes with the same letter or pitch name

    b. Pitches are arranged on the keyboard from A to G before beginning the musical alphabet again

    c. Patterns of seven notes within an octave are called SCALES

    d. The octave can be broken down into twelve half steps resulting in the CHROMATIC SCALES

    e. Patterns of whole steps and half steps determine the MODE of a piece or scale

    f. The most common modes are MAJOR and MINOR

VII. Tonality and Atonality

A. Tonality or Key

1. The most stable sound of a scale or melody

2. Established in comparison with other notes of the scale

3. Called the TONAL CENTER

4. Gives a sense of pitch dominance in a hierarchy

B. The move from an established tonal center creates tension

1. Moving from one tonal center to another is called MODULATION

2. Changing the half step/whole step pattern of an established tonal center achieves modulation

3. Modulation creates tension or instability

VIII. Tonic and Dominant (p. 43)

    A. Chords built on different scale degrees have varying levels of stability

        1. The most important chord is the home chord or TONIC (I)

        2. The next most important chord is the DOMINANT (V)

            a. Announces or prepares the return of the tonic

            b. Dominant to tonic progression provides a sense of completion or relaxation

            c. The end or a phrase is called a CADENCE

            d. An extended cadence at the end of a large work is called a CODA

        3. Other chords have a sense of resolution, though not as strong as the dominant to tonic relation

        4. The motion away from the tonic and the return to the tonic provides the principal harmonic foundation for many large works

IX. The Move from Tonality to Atonality

    A. Occurred in the late 19th century

        1. Composers were required to avoid tonal centers

        2. Composers began to use all twelve notes of the CHROMATIC SCALE

            a. No single note is emphasized over another

            b. Eliminates whole steps in scales

            c. Negates major and minor modes

    B. A work based on chromatic half step relationships is called ATONAL

EXERCISES

1. Working with five to seven classmates, create a brief musical compositon that explores MOTION, PITCH, TONE, HARMONY and TEXTURE. DO NOT USE MUSICAL INSTRUMENTS. Instead, devise your own instruments, such as clapping hands, patting tables or other surfaces as percussion, stretching and plucking rubber bands or buzzing your lips as melodic and harmonic instruments, shuffling your feet in a rhythm, and so on.

2. In conjunction with the above exercise, invent notation symbols to indicate when certain events in your composition are supposed to occur. Write a short description of your compositon and include an explanation of your notational symbols.

3. Listen to the Farandole from *L'Arlésienne Suite* by Georges Bizet. In an essay, describe how Bizet uses different tone colors and instrument families to achieve different textures and ultimately shapes the entire piece. Using drawn symbols or colored pencils make a map of the textures in the Farandole to support your written commentary.

STUDY QUESTIONS

1. Composers manipulate musical elements to fill _music____ space__. (p. 32)

2. Musical motion consists of (p. 32)

   A. Frequency and orchestration

   B. Rhythm and meter

   C. Instrumental color and tempo

   D. Frequency and range

3. Pitch consists of (p. 32)

   A. Frequency and orchestration

   B. Rhythm and meter

   C. Instrumental color and tempo

   D. Frequency and range

4. Texture is the result of varying degrees of _simultaneous activity_ (p. 32)

5. Rhythm is measured by an audible or implied unit called (p. 33)

   A. Timbre

   B. Accent

   C. Beat

   D. Metric foot

6. What defines the meter of a piece of music? (p.33)

   ___how we group the beats_____

7. A measure is a rhythmic unit that contains a specific number of beats. (p. 33)

   A. True

   B. False

8. Meter is represented in notation by the key signature. (p. 33)

   A. True

   B. False

9. Pitch is important in defining the _range__ of each musical instrument. (p. 34)

10. The four elements that make up the sound of a pitch are _attack___, _decay___, _sustain_____, and _release___. (p. 34)

11. The above four elements of a pitch are collectively referred to as (p. 34)

    A. Range

    B. Envelope

    C. Accentuation

    D. Articulation

12. A logical progression of pitches that expresses a musical thought is called _Melody_ (p. 34)

13. The melody type that moves by step or small intervals is called _Conjunct_ (p. 34)

14. The melody type that moves by large intervals is called _Disjunct_ (p. 34)

15. Symbols placed above or below a note to indicated special emphasis for that note are called _Articulation_ markings. (p. 35)

16. A dot placed above or below a note head means for that note to be played (p. 35)

    A. Short and separate from other notes

    B. Double its time value

    C. Smoothly connected to other notes

    D. With a slight vibration added to the tone

17. The sound of a single instrument can be changed by adding the sound of a second instrument. (p. 36)

    A. True

    B. False

18. The manipulation of tone colors can also affect

    A. Meter and rhythm

    B. Texture and range

    C. Texture and harmony

    D. Meter and harmony

19. The process of assigning specific instruments to particular musical ideas is called _orcrestration_. (p. 36)

20. The speed at which the music is played is referred to as (p. 36)

    A. Meter

    B. Tempo

    C. Key

    D. Dynamics

21. The volume level at which the music is played is referred to as (p. 36)

    A. Meter

    B. Tempo

    C. Key

    D. Dynamics

22. Speed and volume level alone can change the character of a composition. (p. 36)

   A. True
   B. False

23. Changes in volume can be used to add drama to melodies and to change musical _Texture_. (p. 36)

24. The Italian term for "soft" is _Piano_. (p. 36)

25. The Italian term for "loud" is _Forte_. (p. 36)

26. The Italian term for "very loud" is _Fortessimo_. (p. 37)

27. The relationship between volume levels creates the difference between loud and soft. (p. 37)

   A. True
   B. False

28. Tempos are indicated by terms that are precisely defined such as *allegro* or *grave*. (p. 37)

   A. True
   B. False

29. The device used by musicians to determine the number of beats per minute in a piece of music is called _metronome_. (p. 37)

30. Which of the following indicate slow tempo markings? (p. 37)

   A. Presto and Vivace
   B. Largo and Adagio
   C. Largo and Presto
   D. Allegro and Adagio

31. Which of the following indicate fast tempo markings? (p. 37)

   A. Presto and Vivace
   B. Largo and Adagio
   C. Largo and Presto
   D. Allegro and Adagio

32. The combination of three of more notes results in a _chord_. (p. 38)

33. Dissonant chords contain notes that blend well with each other. (p. 38)

   A. True
   B. False

34. The relationships between consonant and dissonant chords establish a pattern of _tension_ and resolution. (p. 38)

35. Changing chords that occur with some regularity in a composition create a pattern called _Harmonic rythm_. (p. 38)

36. A phrase is the musical equivalent of a spoken sentence or a thought. (p. 38)

   A. *(circled)* True

   B. False

37. As each musical element intensifies, there is an increase in the overall _____texture____. (p. 38)

38. A single melody sung or played with no accompaniment is called (p. 38)

   A. *(circled)* Monophony

   B. Homophony

   C. Polyphony

39. Two or more independent melodies performed simultaneously is called (p. 38)

   A. Monophony

   B. Homophony

   C. *(circled)* Polyphony

40. A single melody that is supported or accompanied by chords is called (p. 38)

   A. Monophony

   B. *(circled)* Homophony

   C. Polyphony

41. Why would symbols for musical notation need to change? (p. 39)

   _____new sounds discovered_____

42. A sharp sign ___raises___ a pitch by a half step. (p. 41)

43. A flat sign ___lowers___ a pitch by a half step. (p. 41)

44. The above changes to a pitch are called (p. 41)

   A. Alterations

   B. Articulations

   C. *(circled)* Accidentals

   D. Alliteration

45. The distance between any two notes in a melody or a chord is (p. 41)

   A. An octave

   B. A spatial

   C. A half step

   D. *(circled)* An interval

46. The distance between two notes with the same letter name is (p. 42)

   A. *(circled)* An octave

   B. A spatial

   C. A half step

   D. An interval

47. Patterns of seven notes on which compositions are based are called ___scales___. (p. 42)

48. The location of half steps and whole steps in the above seven-note patterns determine the _mode_ of a piece of music (p. 42)

49. The most common modes in western music are _major_ and _minor_ (p. 42)

50. The single note that exhibits a sense of stability compared with other notes in a scale is called (p. 42)

    A.   The octave

    B.   The tonic

    C.   The chromatic

    D.   The dominant

51. A sense of hierarchical pitch relationship is referred to as _tonality or key_ (p. 42)

52. The process of moving from one key area to another is called transmigration. (p. 43)

    A.   True

    B.   False

53. The most stable chord in a key area is called (p. 43)

    A.   The octave

    B.   The tonic

    C.   The chromatic

    D.   The dominant

54. The next most important chord in a hierarchical pitch relationship is (p. 43)

    A.   The octave

    B.   The tonic

    C.   The chromatic

    D.   The dominant

55. The function of the chord listed in question 54 above is to prepare the arrival of the most important chord in a key area. (p. 43)

    A.   True

    B.   False

56. The ending point of a piece of music that provides a sense of completion is called the _Cadence_. (p. 43)

57. The extended ending passage of a large movement is called (p. 43)

    A.   The cadence

    B.   The conclusion

    C.   The coda

    D.   The conjunction

58. The scale that divides the octave into twelve equal half steps is called the _Chromatic_ scale. (p. 44)

59. Music in which a key area is absent or avoided is called _Atonal_. (p. 44)

CHAPTER 4, MUSICAL ARCHITECTURE

This final chapter of Part I considers one of the most important aspects of musical composition: FORM or MUSICAL ARCHITECTURE. The preceding chapters have discussed the many basic elements of music. With form, the composer presents these various elements in combination--rhythm, melody, harmony, and so on--and presents the listener with a variety of sound, yet with an underlying feeling of unity. The author compares a successful musical composition with the three stages of a journey: 1) the excitement of travel, 2) the experience of new and exciting environments, and 3) the return home to familiar surroundings.

The basic elemental unit of form is REPETITION and CONTRAST. This chapter discusses small forms and large forms, and how these forms are utilized by composers in multimovement works. There is also discussion of polyphonic forms and the visual element of music performance.

I. Small Forms (pp. 45-46)

    A. Important elements are REPETITION and CONTRAST

        1. REPETITION

            a. Builds familiarity and stability

            b. A repetition may be exact (AA) or varied (AA')

            c. A varied repetition may repeat a melody with new words or may slightly alter the melody

        2. CONTRAST

            a. Adds interest to the music

            b. Emphasizes a sense of return when the original melody returns

    B. Small forms

        1. BINARY FORM (AB)

            a. A two-part form with contrasting melodies

            b. Both sections are often repeated (AABB)

        2. TERNARY FORM (ABA)

            a. A three-part form with contrast and return

            b. Often used as a form for SONGS (AA'BA)

            c. Middle section (B) often called a BRIDGE

II. Large Forms and Multimovement Works (pp. 47-50)

    A. Many large musical compositions consist of several smaller sections or MOVEMENTS

        1. Each movement is a complete form in itself

        2. Often, movements are thematically related in a large multimovement work

        3. Length and character of movements vary considerably

B.   Standard Large Structures (see Chart p. 47)

    1.   Instrumental structures

        a.   Symphony

        b.   Suite

        c.   Sonata

        d.   Concerto

    2.   Vocal structures

        a.   Cantata

        b.   Oratorio

        c.   Opera

        d.   Liturgical Mass

        e.   Passion

C.   Large movements need contrast and repetition

    1.   Generally more melodic repetitions than small forms

    2.   More opportunity for contrasting themes

    3.   TRANSITIONS between sections may introduce new themes (TRANSITIONAL THEMES)

    4.   Cadences are often extended to allow time for the large movement to come to a rest

D.   THEME AND VARIATIONS (p. 49, fig. 4-2)

    1.   A fundamental and familiar form

    2.   Theme is stated and then changed in each repetition

    3.   Melody may become unrecognizable

    4.   Final statement or variation is often the most similar to the original theme

    5.   Scope and diversity of the variations depend on the imagination and skill of the composer

    6.   Harmonic structure generally remains constant in each variation

    7.   Diagram: A   A1   A2   A3   A4   (etc.)

E.   RONDO (p. 49, fig. 4-3)

    1.   Based on repetitions of a single theme that are separated by contrasting themes

    2.   Contrasting themes serve as bridges between repetitions of the first theme

    3.   Some contrasting themes may be repeated

    4.   Diagrams:

        a.   A   B   A   C   A   D   A

        b.   A   B   A   C   A   B   A

F.   SONATA-ALLEGRO (SONATA; pp. 49-50, fig. 4-4)

    1.   A large TERNARY form (A   B   A')

    2.   Each section has its own name and character

        a.   EXPOSITION (A)

         i.   Has two themes or THEME GROUPS

         ii. First theme is in the tonic key

         iii. Second theme is in the dominant key (or relative major if a minor tonic)

   b. DEVELOPMENT (B)

         i.   Either or both themes are extensively reworked

         ii. Contains much modulation and rhythmic diversity

         iii. Very unstable harmonically

         iv. Drives to the dominant to set up next section

   c. RECAPITULATION (A')

         i.   Restates both themes or group

         ii. All themes remain in the tonic key

  3. In the 19th century the final cadence was extended, creating a long, dramatic CODA

G. MINUET AND TRIO (p. 50, fig. 4-5)

  1. Based on an early dance form in triple meter

  2. A large ternary form (A   B   A')

  3. Minuet (A, A'), Trio (B) were originally two separate dances

   a. Each dance is a binary form (A B)

   b. Each section is repeated

   c. Repeats are usually not observed in the return of the Minuet (A')

  4. Several contrasting points between Minuet and Trio

   a. Minuet in tonic, Trio in a related key

   b. Trio is usually quieter, more flowing melody

   c. Rhythms may be different although meter remains in triple meter

   d. Orchestration may vary in the Trio

  5. Changed to SCHERZO AND TRIO after 1800

   a. Form remained the same

   b. Tempo increased a great deal

III. Contrapuntal or Polyphonic Forms (pp. 51-54)

A. Characteristics of COUNTERPOINT

  1. Two or more melodies that:

   a. Accompany each other

   b. Retain some amount of independence

   c. Each melodic line can stand on its own

  2. Two principal types of counterpoint

   a. Imitative--melodies are exact or similar repetitions

   b. Nonimitative--melodies are not related to each other

B. Common imitative contrapuntal forms

    1. CANON (p. 51)

        a. Overlapping of the same melody

        b. One part begins alone, other parts begin later

        c. Example: Row, Row, Row Your Boat

    2. PASSACAGLIA (p. 51, fig. 4-6)

        a. Based on a repeated GROUND BASS (BASSO OSTINATO)

        b. Uses repetition rather than imitation

            i. New melodies in upper voices over repeated bass line

            ii. Number of repetitions determined by composer

            iii. Very few or no changes in the bass melody of each repetition

    3. FUGUE (pp. 51-52, fig. 4-7)

        a. Very thick musical texture

        b. May use both imitative and nonimitative melodies

        c. Begins with single voice stating SUBJECT (main theme)

        d. Second voice follows with a similar ANSWER

        e. Other voices alternate subject and answer

        f. May make use of a COUNTERSUBJECT against statements of subjects or answers

        g. Sections built of subjects and answers may be separated by free sections

            i. Often modulates to related keys

            ii. May contain fragments of the subject, answer, or countersubject

        h. LISTENING NOTES: Benjamin Britten, *The Young Person's Guide to the Orchestra, Op. 34* (pp. 52-54)

IV. Visual Elements in Musical Performance (pp. 54-55)

  A. Visual elements help organize musical events

  B. The CONDUCTOR

    1. Uses body motions to interpret the music

    2. Informs the performers and the audience of the important themes and rhythms

    3. Interprets tempos and dynamics

    4. See conducting patterns in fig. 4-8 (p. 54)

  C. DANCE

    1. Informs the audience of rhythmic accents and flowing melodies

    2. All dances require specific rhythms

    3. Music accompanies movement while movement accompanies the music

  D. OPERA/MUSICAL THEATER

    1. Story line used to unify musical themes

    2. Music enriches and helps to define emotions

    3. Film music can also be considered in this category

  E. MUSIC VIDEOS

    1. Wide spectrum of scenes and effects

    2. Combines music, dance, and stagecraft with musical and visual special effects

    3. While most songs can stand on their own, a song's success is often determined by the link between audio and video

EXERCISES

1. Listen to the song "When I am laid in earth" from the opera *Dido and Aeneas* by Henry Purcell. Pay close attention to the bass line under the vocal part; this is an example of a GROUND BASS. Describe this ground bass and create a graphic map to show the shape of this bass line. How many times is this bass melody repeated in the aria? How does the bass line fit with the vocal melody?

2. Listen to one of the following pieces: Piano Concerto in G major, K. 453, 3rd movement, by Mozart; Symphony No. 103 in E-flat major, 2nd movement, by Haydn; or Quintet in A major, 4th movement ("The Trout"), by Schubert. Describe in a brief essay the changes that occur in each variation of the theme. Is one variation more effective than the others? Why is this, or how does the composer achieve this? Which variation seems to get the furthest away from the original theme?

3. Select three music videos to critique. They may be videos that you really like or that are very effective or they may be videos that you really dislike. How are music, stagecraft, and dance combined to create the total video experience? Does what is on the screen match with what is in the lyrics of the song? Would the song be just as effective without the video? Why or why not?

STUDY QUESTIONS

1. Name two reasons why music compositions need structure. (p. 45)

  A. *allow for diversity in sound*

  B. *give feeling of unity to a work*

2. Megill compares the structure of a successful musical composition with (p. 45)

  A. The stages of a film

  B. The stages of a vacation

  C. The stages of a novel

  D. The stages of life

3. The most important factors in musical structure are _repetition_ and _contrast_. (p. 45)

4. Diagram a ternary structure (p. 46): _ABA_

5. Diagram a binary structure (p. 46): _AB_

6. The middle section of a song that has a new text and new melody is called

   A.   The transition

   B.   The song cycle

   C.   The bridge

   D.   The song form

7. A large work such as a symphony is made up of smaller sections called _movements_. (p. 47)

8. Each smaller section named above is a complete musical structure in itself. (p. 47)

   A.   True

   B.   False

9. Which of the following large forms are similar to the opera? (p. 47)

   A.   Oratorio and Passion

   B.   Passion and Symphony

   C.   Cantata and Suite

   D.   Sonata and Symphony

10. Which of the following large forms are instrumental genres? (p. 47)

   A.   Oratorio and Passion

   B.   Passion and Symphony

   C.   Cantata and Suite

   D.   Sonata and Symphony

11. Unlike small forms, large forms do not use repetition and contrast to unify the whole work. (p. 48)

   A.   True

   B.   False

12. A short melodic sequence that provides progression between larger musical ideas is called a _transitional_ theme (p. 48)

13. Why are cadences and endings of large works often extended by the composer? (p. 48)
   allow work to unwind and come to rest

14. In a theme and variation movement the harmonic structure generally remains the same. (p. 49)

   A.   True

   B.   False

15. Themes are often varied to the point that they are unrecognizable. (p. 49)

   A.   True

   B.   False

16. Diagram a seven-part rondo form (p. 49): _ABACADA_

29

17. The structural principle of the rondo is alternation of the original theme with similar themes. (p. 49)

    A.   True

    B.   False

18. The overall structure of sonata-allegro form is (p. 49)

    A.   Binary

    B.   Rondo

    C.   Ternary

    D.   Fugal

19. In a sonata-allegro form the _Exposition_ consists of two theme groups, the first in the tonic and the second in a related key. (p. 49)

20. What is the purpose of the development section in a sonata-allegro form? (p. 50)

Break down themes into smaller units & Change key

21. The technique of changing keys in a piece of music is called _modulation_ (p. 50)

22. In the recapitulation the first theme is presented in the tonic and the second theme is presented in a related key. (p. 50)

    A.   True

    B.   False

23. In the 19th century the final cadence of a sonata-allegro form was extended to become the _Coda_. (p. 50)

24. The minuet and trio is characterized by its dance form in _triple_ meter. (p. 50)

25. The overall form of the minuet and trio is a _ternary_ form. (p. 50)

26. The form of a minuet or a trio by itself is a _Binary_ form. (p. 50)

27. In the 19th century the minuet and trio was replaced by the _Scherzo_ and trio. (p. 50)

28. The technique of writing multiple melodies that remain relatively independent is called _Counterpoint_. (p. 51)

29. The most common imitative form is

    A.   Fugue

    B.   Canon

    C.   Passacaglia

    D.   Ground bass

30. Another term for the repeated bass line in a passacaglia is _Ground Bass_. (p. 51)

31. The melodic material in a passacaglia consists of repeated material over a changing bass line. (p. 51)

    A.   True

    B.   False

32. The fugue uses imitative and nonimitative techniques. (p. 51)

    A. True

    B. False

33. The principal theme of a fugue is called _Subject_. (p. 52)

34. The second voice that follows the above-named theme is called _Answer_. (p. 52)

35. The complementary melody that supplies new motives to a fugue is called
    Countersubject. (p. 52)

36. The conductor will shape the music by (p.54)

    A. Improvising on the piano or violin

    B. Varying the tempo and dynamics

    C. Changing the order of the movements

    D. Asking the audience to hold their applause

37. In what way does music interact with dance to create a visual element? (p. 54)

    _____

38. Dances like the mazurka, the waltz, the sarabande, and the fox trot all have similar rhythms. (p. 55)

    A. True

    B. False

39. A dramatic production that is based on everyday themes and has vocal and instrumental sounds
    that are related to traditional musical styles is called _musical theatre_. (p. 55)

40. The meaning of some music videos comes from the visual aspect of the performance. (p. 55)

    A. True

    B. False

41. Music videos combine music, _Dance_, and _Stagecraft_ with specialized
    musical and visual effects. (p. 55)

CHAPTER 5, THE MEDIEVAL/GOTHIC PERIOD: Extant to 1450

    This chapter deals with the music of the MEDIEVAL or GOTHIC period in Western Europe. This period, roughly from 500 to 1450 A.D., produced the earliest examples of musical notation. While it is known that earlier civilizations used music, especially for religious ceremonies, music historians can only guess the nature of such activities from writings, statuary, and paintings.

    In the medieval period, the most important social institutions were the Catholic Church and the feudal systems of Europe. Both institutions used music for both ceremony and entertainment, but it was primarily in the church that music was written down and preserved in notational form. Most of the secular, or nonchurch, music of the time was not notated and much has been lost. Consequently, since the church musicians preserved the music they used every day, most of the existing music of the medieval period is sacred music.

    I. Medieval Music: Early Sacred Music (pp. 59-62)

      A. The earliest type of sacred music was CHANT

          1. GREGORIAN CHANT

              a. Single-line, unaccompanied melody (MONOPHONY)

              b. Latin sacred text

              c. Accompanied parts of religious service (MASS)

              d. Collected by order of Pope Gregory I

          2. Chants demonstrate the importance of melodic construction for composers

          3. Supply the musical material for other original compositions for the next several hundred years

          4. Other chant types

              a. BYZANTINE

              b. AMBROSIAN

      B. Notational system developed between 900 and 1100 A.D.

          1. Ornate system representing melodic shapes

          2. Did not include ornaments added in performance

          3. Rhythms are flexible, fluid, flowing

      C. Chant melodies were based on the CHURCH MODES

          1. Scales consisting of patterns of whole steps and half steps

          2. Each mode is identified according to the positions of half steps and whole steps

          3. Two of the church modes evolved into our major and minor scales

      D. Some chants are MELISMATIC

          1. Several notes sung to one text syllable (MELISMA)

2. Some melismas are very long

E. Chant is the oldest type of music with a specific notational system that can be performed today

    1. Although very old, chant has never left our culture

    2. Several churches still use chant in the most important services

    3. Chant has the longest traditional existence of any musical style

F. LISTENING NOTES: Introit, *Gaudeamus* (pp. 60-61)

II. The Move to Polyphony (pp. 62-65)

A. Polyphony developed slowly out of homophonic music

    1. Men and boys performed chant in church services

    2. Boys naturally sang an octave higher than the men

    3. Melodies moved in parallel octaves

    4. Eventually added a second consonant interval

        a. Added a fifth above the melody

        b. The fifth was a natural consonance derived from the overtone series (see Chap. 1)

B. PARALLEL ORGANUM (fig. 5-1, p. 62)

    1. The first type of polyphony

    2. All singers begin on the same note

    3. Part of the group would sing up to the desired consonant interval

    4. Both groups of singers would sing in parallel motion at this interval until a cadence point

    5. The upper melody was probably originally improvised

    6. Notated organum was very precise in performance

C. FREE ORGANUM (fig. 5-2, p. 63)

    1. The next step in the development of polyphony

    2. Independence of parts appeared first in improvisation, then in composition

    3. Both parts are free to move in opposite or parallel directions

    4. As in parallel organum, both parts changed notes at the same time

D. MELISMATIC ORGANUM (fig. 5-3, p. 63)

    1. Followed free organum to more independent parts

    2. Upper part freely added several notes above each text syllable in the lower part

    3. Lower part usually had one long note against the upper MELISMA

E. The importance of chant continued throughout the development of polyphony

    1. Beginning in the early 12th century, chant was the basis for new compositions

    2. CANTUS FIRMUS (FIXED SONG)

        a. A pre-existing chant or part of a chant

        b. Placed in the lowest voice part (TENOR)

        c. New melodies (DUPLUM) were written to be sung over the cantus firmus

        d.   Cantus firmus was at first like a drone beneath the new melodies

        e.   Composers began to alter the cantus firmus to make the parts more equal to each other

    3.   Eventually three and four parts were written

F.   The most important center in the development of polyphony was the Cathedral of Notre Dame, Paris

    1.   Notre Dame School flourished about 1150

    2.   Developed a system of MEASURED RHYTHM

        a.   Clear system of metered music

        b.   Each beat divided into three pulses

        c.   Symbolized the Trinity of the Catholic Church

        d.   Rhythmic precision added new motion to the music

    3.   LISTENING NOTES: Leonin, *Alleluia Dies Sanctificatus* (excerpt; p. 65)

III. Ars Nova (pp. 65-67)

A.   French and Italian music of the 14th century reflected several social factors

    1.   Secular music was combined with sacred music

    2.   Emphasized realism and secular emotions

    3.   The slow chant cantus firmus was replaced by secular popular or folk songs

        a.   Drinking songs

        b.   Songs with animal sounds

    4.   The original Latin text was replaced by texts in French or Italian

B.   The new, popular polyphonic style was called ARS NOVA (NEW ART)

C.   Presented new conceptions in music composition

    1.   More precise manner of notation

    2.   Triple rhythms of the Notre Dame School were further subdivided into two pulses

    3.   Use of SYNCOPATION (accenting between the beats) became more common

    4.   Important vocal forms include

        a.   The polyphonic MOTET

        b.   The LITURGICAL MASS

            i.   ORDINARY

                1.   Performed every day with no changes

                2.   Very repetitive, severe

                3.   Little or no ornamentation to voice parts

           ii.   PROPER

                1.   Text changed every day according to church season

                2.   Generally more expressive music than is found in the ordinary

5. GUILLAUME DE MACHAUT (see biography, p. 66)

    a. A famous musician and poet

    b. Considered the first composer to write a complete polyphonic setting of the mass ordinary

    c. LISTENING NOTES: "Agnus Dei I" from the *Messe de Notre Dame* (p. 67)

EXERCISES

1. Listen to a recording of a Gregorian chant, other than the one included on the tape set. Describe the character of the music that you hear. How would you describe the musical style of the performance? How does this music make you feel? Make a graphic map of the melodic shape. At what points on the map do you have a sense of a tonic?

2. Using only the white keys on the piano, play the following octave scale ranges: D to D, E to E, F to F, and G to G. These are the CHURCH MODES discussed earlier in this chapter. Which modes are similar? Which modes resemble the major or minor scales? What are the patterns of whole steps and half steps in each mode? Between what scale degrees do the half steps occur in each mode? Select one mode that you like the sound of and compose a short melody using just the pitches in that mode and imitating the chanting style of the examples you have heard.

3. In your school or public library, look for two recorded examples of secular songs from the 14th century, one by Guillaume de Machaut (like a MOTET) and one by Francesco Landini (like a BALLATA). (There are several good recordings of these composers' music available on compact discs.) While listening to each example, compare or contrast what you are hearing. Besides the obvious difference in languages, what are you hearing? Is rhythm used in a similar way by each composer? What about the accompaniment, if any? In what ways are the melodies similar to chant melodies? In what way are they different? If the recordings provide a translation of the text (most do), how do the subject matter of these songs compare with one another? Write up your findings in a brief one or two page essay.

STUDY QUESTIONS

1. In ancient times all art practices were handed down to the next generation through (p. 58)

    A. Notation

    B. Hieroglyphs

    C. Folklore

    D. Explicit written instructions

2. Much ancient music is classified today as high art because it is so old. (p. 58)

    A. ⟲ True

    B. False

3. A people's history was often communicated through _Song_ and _Chant_ (p. 58)

4. The practice of providing a record of historical events in ancient times is often through _Oral_ tradition. (p. 58)

5. Scientists have learned much about how music may have been used in ancient times by studying the music of _Aboriginal_ tribes today. (p. 59)

6. Why does music have the shortest documented history of all the fine arts? (p. 59)
    no system of notation existed.

7. Name two sources that historians have used to surmise the nature of musical activities before about 500 A.D. (p. 59)

    A. _Pictures_

    B. _Wall Sketches_

8. Why is more sacred music than secular music available for study today? (p. 59)
    It was passed down by Churches.

9. The texture of Gregorian chant is (p. 59)

    A. Imitative polyphony

    B. ⟲ Monophonic

    C. Melodic

    D. Homophonic

10. Gregorian chant is so called because (p. 59)

    A. It was composed by the monk Gregory of Ghent

    B. It was composed by Pope Gregory I

    C. It was discovered in modern times in the tomb of St. Gregory of Tours

    D. ⟲ It was ordered collected and standardized by Pope Gregory I

11. Two other types of church chant were _Byzantine_ and _Ambrosian_. (p. 59)

12. Why is the study of chant important? (p. 59)

13. Which of the following is NOT characteristic of chant? (p. 59)

    A. It is unaccompanied

    B. ⟲ It has a definite meter

    C. It has an ornate melody

    D. It has flexible and fluid rhythms

14. The notation of chant was so specific as to include the free ornaments that were used in performance. (p. 59)

    A. True
    B. False

15. Chant melodies are based on _modes_. (p. 60)

16. A chant melody that has several notes placed over a single text syllable is called (p. 60)

    A. A melisma
    B. A mode
    C. A melissa
    D. A miasma

17. Why has chant had the longest traditional existence of any musical style? (p. 62)

    It has been passed down by Churches

18. The change from a single-line melody to two or more melodies happened very quickly. (p. 62)

    A. True
    B. False

19. What may have caused the first step in polyphonic singing? (p. 62)

    Boys singing a melody 1 octave higer than men

20. A two-part form of early polyphony is called _Organum_. (p. 62)

21. The type of polyphony in which two voice-parts moved as one at a constant interval is (p. 62)

    A. Paralegal organum
    B. Parallel organum
    C. Paradigm organum
    D. Paraclete organum

22. Briefly describe free organum. (p. 63) _2 voice parts move in opposite directions or parallel_

23. The type of polyphony in which the upper voice added several melody notes above one note in the lower part is called (p. 63)

    A. Mellifluous organum
    B. Melanomic organum
    C. Melismatic organum
    D. Melodious organum

24. A chant or chant segment that was used as the basis for a new composition was called a _Cantus Firmus_. (p.63)

25. The borrowed melody named in number 24 above was placed in which voice? (p. 63)

    tenor

26. The church was at first skeptical about polyphonic music because of the increase of dissonance. (p. 63)

   Ⓐ. True

   B. False

27. The borrowed chant melody might be altered by the composer in order to (pp. 63-64)

   __minimizing contrast making parts nearly equal.__

28. The center of musical activity in the 12th century is known as the School of __Notre Dame__. (p. 64)

29. The notational system associated with the above named school is called (p. 64)

   A. Mitered rhythm

   B. Organum rhythm

   Ⓒ. Measured rhythm

   D. Odd rhythm

30. The choirmasters associated with this school are __Leonin__ and __Perotin__. (p. 64)

31. The basic beat of these composers' music was divided into three parts and symbolized the __Trinity__. (p. 64)

32. The music period of 14th century France and Italy is called the (p. 66)

   A. Secular Art

   B. Sacred Art

   C. Polyphonic Art

   Ⓓ. New Art

33. The borrowed chant melodies were replaced by popular songs (p 65)

   Ⓐ. True

   B. False

34. A new type of polyphonic song that became popular in this period was the __Motet__. (p. 66)

35. The technique in which an accent is placed on a beat that is normally not accented is called

   A. Specialization

   Ⓑ. Syncopation

   C. Solmization

   D. Sedentation

36. The section of the liturgical mass that is performed at every service and never changes is called the __Ordinary__. (p.66)

37. The other major part of the liturgical mass (the part that changes) is called the __Proper__. (p. 67)

38. A major poet/composer of 14th century France was (p. 66)

    A.   Gilles de Rais

    B.   Leonin de Paris

    C.   Guillaume de Machaut

    D.   Lucienne de Provence

39. The first significant setting of a mass by one composer was the Mass of _Notre Dame_ by _Machaut_. (p. 66)

CHAPTER 6, THE RENAISSANCE PERIOD 1450-1600

In the style period known as the Renaissance ("Rebirth"), most music was composed for vocal ensembles. The polyphony that began to develop in the medieval period culminated in the intricate imitative polyphonic motet of the Renaissance masters such as Josquin Desprez and Giovanni da Palestrina. The motet and the mass were the principal sacred music genres of the Renaissance. In secular music, the imitative style of the motet was used to create the principal secular vocal genre, the madrigal.

Historically and culturally, the Renaissance was one of the great periods of Western Europe. It was the Age of Exploration, in which several European monarchies extended their borders to include the newly discovered lands across the sea. The period also produced some of the greatest artists the world has ever known, such as Leonardo da Vinci, Michelangelo, Raphael, Donatello, Rembrandt, and a host of other painters, sculptors, and architects. This period also gave rise to the great Reformation in the 16th century and the rise of several Protestant faiths that challenged the supremacy of the Catholic Church.

I. The Motet (pp. 69-73)

    A. By 1450 polyphonic music featured independent melodies

    B. An important compositional technique was IMITATION

        1. Each voice part repeated or imitated a melody

        2. Melodies were not strictly or exactly imitated

        3. There was some sense of freedom in the voice parts

        4. The beginning of each text phrase was called a POINT OF IMITATION

            a. All parts would enter in turn

            b. Melodies would overlap and imitate each other

            c. Served to unify each phrase of the text

            d. Most melodic freedom appeared at cadence points

    C. Composers favored the MOTET

        1. Polyphonic choral work

        2. Used sacred Latin text

        3. Performed A CAPPELLA, with no accompaniment

        4. Not LITURGICAL; not based on Mass texts

        5. Voice parts are considered CONTRAPUNTAL

            a. Each melody has its own musical character

            b. Each part can be heard clearly against the others

            c. Was referred to by composers as Point (Note) Against Point (Latin: PUNCTUS CONTRAPUNCTUS)

        6. Best show Renaissance composers' interest in imitation and intricate polyphony

7. JOSQUIN DESPREZ (see biography, p. 69)

   a. Wrote very graceful, flowing melodies

   b. The most important of the early motet composers

   c. LISTENING NOTES: *Ave Christie immolate* (pp. 70-71)

D. Choral church music was challenged in the mid-16th century as not being serious enough for the Mass

   1. Important restrictions were placed on church composers by the COUNCIL OF TRENT

   2. Composers encouraged to use CANTUS FIRMUS techniques with chant melodies (rather than secular melodies)

   3. GIOVANNI PIERLUIGI DA PALESTRINA (see biography, p. 72)

      a. Helped create a more conservative, polyphonic style of writing

      b. Showed that polyphony could present the text clearly

      c. Palestrina's style is considered to be fluid and nearly tonal

      d. LISTENING NOTES: "Kyrie eleison" from the *Pope Marcellus Mass* (p. 73)

II. The Madrigal (pp. 76-78)

A. An important type of renaissance secular song

B. Similar to the motet

   1. Uses imitation techniques

   2. Contrasts polyphonic and homophonic textures

   3. Uses WORD PAINTING

      a. Using music to emphasize a certain word or idea

      b. Emphasis interprets the meaning of the word

      c. Sometimes referred to as MADRIGALISMS

C. Different from the motet

   1. Uses the vernacular language (Italian or English)

   2. Text deals with secular topics

   3. Performed at home and at social gatherings

D. Two important types were Italian and English

   1. English madrigal also called BALLET

      a. Homophonic verse with polyphonic REFRAIN

      b. Refrains consisted of complex "fa-la-las"

      c. LISTENING NOTES: Thomas Morley, *Now Is the Month of Maying* (p. 77)

   2. An important Italian madrigal composer was Carlo Gesualdo

      a. Music uses word painting to the extreme

      b. Gesualdo's madrigals are very dramatic

      c. Melodies are very chromatic

        d.   Music has very strong emotional tendencies

  E. The CHANSON (SONG)

     1. French secular polyphonic song

     2. Strong rhythmic accents

     3. Generally very repetitive

     4. Important chanson composer was Guillaume DuFay

     5. LISTENING NOTES: Clement Jannequin, *Song of the Birds* (Topic 3, pp. 229-230)

  F. The LIED (SONG)

     1. German secular polyphonic song

     2. Imitates the madrigal and chanson in style

III. Instrumental and Polychoral Motets (pp. 78-80)

  A. Instrumental music in the Renaissance was derived primarily from vocal music

     1. Accompanied vocal performances

     2. Instruments usually DOUBLED or played the same melody as the voices

     3. Instruments were grouped in families or CONSORTS

         a. Four instruments of the same family and timbre

         b. Parallel the voice ranges: soprano, alto, tenor, and bass

  B. The VENETIAN SCHOOL

     1. Developed new styles of instrumental music

     2. Center was St. Mark's cathedral in Venice

     3. An important musical type was the POLYCHORAL MOTET

         a. Two or more choirs in separate choir lofts

         b. Each choir had its own group of accompanists

         c. Imitation would appear between voice parts in each choir and between the choirs in echo effect

     4. Works for instruments alone were performed for large, festive occasions

     5. GIOVANNI GABRIELI (see biography, p. 80)

         a. The most notable composer of the Venetian School

         b. Was a singer and organist at St. Mark's

         c. Equally fluent writing instrumental and vocal music

     6. Instrumental music styles were important in making a transition from the Renaissance to the Baroque

EXERCISES

1. Listen to a recording of the Lutheran hymn *A Mighty Fortress Is Our God* by Martin Luther. Compare this with a motet by Josquin Desprez. How do the voices in each piece relate to one another? How does each composer's treatment of the voices differ? Listen for the following musical elements in each performance: RHYTHM, MELODY, and TEXTURE. Are these elements similar? Are they very different? Which piece sounds the least complex to you?

2. Listen to the madrigals *Moro Lasso* by Carlo Gesualdo and *As Vesta Was Descending* by Thomas Weelkes. Compare the two pieces for such elements as the use of chromatic notes, word painting, emotional quality, drama, and texture. Does one seem more effective than the other in musically describing the text? Why or why not?

3. Using the same criteria as number 2 above, compare the Gesualdo madrigal with the motet *Stabat Mater* by Palestrina. Besides the difference in language and subject matter, how do these two works differ? Does one seem to be more dramatic or emotional than the other? How does the composer achieve this?

STUDY QUESTIONS

1. The new compositional technique in the Renaissance was (p. 69)

    A. Cantus firmus

    B. Imitative polyphony

    C. Monophony

    D. Sonata

2. In canon, all the voice parts sing the melody in turn but with considerable freedom. (p. 69)

    A. True

    B. False

3. In the new Renaissance singing style, each text phrase was sung in turn and called Point of imitation _____. (p. 69)

4. At what point in a Renaissance motet did the greatest amount of freedom in each voice occur? (p. 69)
    _____ Cadences points _____

5. One of the major composers of the new singing style was (p. 69)

    A. Guillaume DuFay

    B. Giovanni Gabrieli

    C. Josquin Desprez

    D. Guillaume de Machaut

6. The texts for Renaissance motets were written in (p. 70)

    A.   French

    B.   Italian

    C.   Flemish

    D.   Latin

7. Motets are sacred works that are based on a section of the Mass. (p. 70)

    A.   True

    B.   False

8. Motets best display Renaissance composers' focus on ___imitatio___ and
    ___polyphony___. (p. 70)

9. Choral music that is performed without accompaniment is called ___a cappella___. (p. 70)

10. A style of polyphonic writing in which all parts can be heard clearly is (p. 70)

    A.   Contrapuntal writing

    B.   Homophonic writing

    C.   Polychoral writing

    D.   Polyrhythmic writing

11. A small ensemble that played instruments of the same family is called (p. 71)

    A.   A construct

    B.   A conduct

    C.   A consort

    D.   A cappella

12. Why would the above named ensemble use instruments of varied sizes? (p. 71)
    ___to get different octave sounds___

13. Church music was challenged by the Catholic Church as being too serious for the liturgy. (p. 72)

    A.   True

    B.   False

14. Church composers were urged to return to using ___cantus firmus___ techniques. (p. 72)

15. The composer who helped shape a more conservative polyphonic style in church music was (p. 72)

    A.   Josquin Desprez

    B.   Giovanni Gabrieli

    C.   Carlo Gesualdo

    D.   Giovanni da Palestrina

16. The form of the Kyrie eleison from the *Pope Marcellus Mass* is (p. 73)

    A.   A A B A

    B.   A B A

    C.   A B A C A

    D.   A B C

17. The type of secular song that was similar to the motet is the _madrigal_. (p. 76)

18. Which of the following is NOT common to both the motet and madrigal? (p. 76)

    A.   Imitation techniques

    B.   Word painting

    C.   Polyphonic and homophonic textures

    D.   Vernacular texts

19. Why was word painting used by Renaissance composers? (p. 76)

    to interpret special meanings of words

20. Specific words or feelings that were musically emphasized and related to word painting
    are called _madrigalisms_. (p. 76)

21. The popular English madrigal style is called the (p. 76)

    A.   English motet

    B.   Lied

    C.   Ballett

    D.   Chanson

22. The English madrigal style typically has a _homophonic_ verse followed by a
    polyphonic refrain of fa-la-la. (p. 76)

23. The Italian madrigal composer whose music is perhaps the most extreme example of word
    painting is (p. 76)

    A.   Josquin Desprez

    B.   Giovanni Gabrieli

    C.   Carlo Gesualdo

    D.   Giovanni da Palestrina

24. The secular French version of the motet style is called the (p. 77)

    A.   French motet

    B.   Lied

    C.   Ballett

    D.   Chanson

25. The French composer whose works best represent the 15th century French style is (p. 77)

A. Guillaume DuFay

B. Giovanni Gabrieli

C. Josquin Desprez

D. Guillaume de Machaut

26. The secular German style of the motet style is called the (p. 78)

A. German motet

B. Lied

C. Ballett

D. Chanson

27. The technique in which two or more voices or instruments perform the same melody at the same time is called _doubling_. (p. 78)

28. The late-16th century group of composers who composed both vocal and instrumental music was the (p. 78)

A. Flemish School

B. Notre Dame School

C. Venetian School

D. English School

29. A main center for the development of the music of the above named group was _St. Marks_ cathedral. (p. 78)

30. A motet performed by more than one choir or group of instruments is called _Polychoral_. (p.78) Motets

31. What architectural feature suggested the development of the above motet style? (p. 78)
Churchs Configuration

32. Works for instruments alone were not performed in the Renaissance. (p. 79)

A. True

B. False

33. The most notable composer of the School named in question 28 above was (pp. 79-80)

A. Guillaume DuFay

B. Giovanni Gabrieli

C. Josquin Desprez

D. Guillaume de Machaut

34. The new perception of instrumental music led to the transition to the _Baroque_ (p.79)

CHAPTER 7, THE BAROQUE PERIOD: 1600 to 1750

The period from about 1600 to 1750 is known as the Baroque period. There are several changes that occur in music history at this time, changes that had been somewhat foreshadowed in the music of the Venetian composers at the end of the 16th century. The music of the previous periods is characterized by the use of the church modes as the basis of melodic structure. Composers in the Baroque became dependent on only two of these church modes, those that we now know as the MAJOR SCALE and the MINOR SCALE. The Baroque period is marked by a gradual shift from MODALITY to TONALITY, to the dependence on a tonic note or tonal center. Composers begin to consider harmonic structure more important in their music, much more important than the linear melodic structure of the Renaissance. They also begin to use a shorthand notational system called FIGURED BASS to tell keyboard players what harmonies are needed to support the melody.

There was much more music being written strictly for instruments in the Baroque period and new instrumental forms were developed by composers to showcase the instrumental musicians with whom they worked. Some new instrumental genres that developed in this period are the TRIO SONATA, the FUGUE, and the CONCERTO. The sonata and the concerto in particular will become very important and popular musical genres well into the 20th century. In vocal music, Italian composers near the end of the 16th century developed a new type of vocal music that includes not only solo singing and instrumental music, but also dancing, choral singing, costuming, and extravagant scenery. This new type of musical entertainment, OPERA, caught on very quickly in 17th century Italy and soon spread to France, Germany, and England. From opera was developed other large vocal genres that were mostly religious in nature-- the ORATORIO, the CANTATA, and the PASSION. Major composers discussed in this chapter are ANTONIO VIVALDI, GEORGE FRIDERIC HANDEL, and JOHANN SEBASTIAN BACH.

I. Detail and Precision (pp. 82-83)

  A. Detail is an important concern in all the arts

    1. Detail unifies a work of art

    2. Detail in artistic thought often creates new but related thoughts

    3. Basic elements and details of a work of art are related to the whole

    4. Emphasis on detail is the essence of the Baroque style

      a. Concern for the expression of emotion

      b. Increased love of contrasting material

      c. Necessary for creating intensely emotional music

  B. Monody, monodic style

    1. New vocal style of solo voice accompanied by BASSO CONTINUO

    2. Developed by a group of poet/musicians--the FLORENTINE CAMERATA

3. Emphasis placed on understanding the words of the text

4. The text is more important than the music

5. Develops into RECITATIVE

    a. Declamatory vocal style

    b. Relates the story line (plot) in an opera

    c. Accompanied by BASSO CONTINUO

    d. Recitative that is accompanied by the basso continuo is called DRY (SECCO) recitative

C. BASSO CONTINUO

1. Strong bass line that supports the melody

2. Provides the harmonic foundation of a piece of music

3. Typically performed by an instrument that can play chords (e.g., harpsichord or lute) and a bass instrument (e.g., cello) that reinforces the bass line; two instrumentalists

D. THOROUGH BASS

1. A bass line that accompanies a melody; basso continuo

2. Numbers placed beneath the notes on the staff

    a. Indicate specific intervals to be played above the bass notes; chords

    b. Allowed keyboardist to improvise an accompaniment to enhance the soloist

    c. Also called FIGURED BASS

E. GROUND BASS (BASSO OSTINATO)

1. Repeated melody in the bass line

2. Supports solo melody that is written above it

3. Repetition serves to unify a piece of music

4. Also called PASSACAGLIA

5. Example: Purcell, aria "Dido's Lament" from *Dido and Aeneas*

II. Opera and Other Related Vocal Forms (pp. 83-92)

A. Developed from the relationship between text, expression, and emotion

B. Opera composers also had to write instrumental segments

1. Overtures, interludes, endings

2. Written to contrast with the vocal sections of the opera

3. Referred to as SINFONIAS

C. The ARIA

1. An emotional solo vocal piece within an opera

2. Intended for the characters to express feelings about a situation (contrast with RECITATIVE)

3. Scored more fully for orchestra and solo voice than is recitative

48

    4.   Opportunity for VIRTUOSO singers to display their skill

    5.   Often described as BEL CANTO (beautiful singing)

    6.   DA CAPO ARIA

        a.   The most popular type of aria in the 17th and 18th centuries

        b.   A ternary (three-part) form--A B A'

        c.   The last section (A') was meant to be heavily ornamented

D.   Principal roles were often performed by CASTRATI

    1.   Male singers castrated before puberty

    2.   Combined the high vocal range of a young boy with the strength, endurance, and experience of a man

    3.   Castrati were highly valued singers, had the most prestige of all singers

E.   Even balance between aria and recitative provides contrast for the opera (see table, p. 87)

F.   CLAUDIO MONTEVERDI (see biography, p. 84)

    1.   One of the major figures in the development of opera

    2.   Composed many vocal works of secular and sacred type

    3.   Composed in both the old Renaissance style and the new Baroque style

    4.   LISTENING NOTES: Recitative "Tu se' morta" and Chorus "Ahi, caso acerbo" from *L'Orfeo* (p. 85)

G.   BALLAD OPERA

    1.   A more popular style of opera attracting audiences from the middle class

    2.   Light and humorous type of opera

    3.   Popular in England especially in the 18th century

    4.   Often made use of the popular songs of the day

    5.   Lead to a decline in the popularity of Italian opera in England

    6.   Example: John Gay, *The Beggar's Opera*

H.   ORATORIO

    1.   A large vocal and instrumental dramatic work based on a sacred subject

    2.   Contains arias, recitatives, and sinfonias (like opera)

    3.   Is not staged or performed in costumes; no dramatic acting

        a.   Less expensive to produce than an opera

        b.   Attracted more diverse audience from the middle class

    4.   Often makes more use of choral singing than of solo singing

        a.   Used to express noble, sacred feelings

        b.   Typically has several voices singing several different parts

        c.   Texture is usually more polyphonic

I. GEORGE FRIDERIC HANDEL (see biography, p. 88)

    1. The most important composer of English oratorio in the 18th century

    2. Was also a master of Italian opera style before his move away to the oratorio

    3. LISTENING NOTES: Recitative "There were shepherds abiding in the field," Chorus "Glory to God," Aria "Rejoice Greatly," Chorus "Hallelujah," and Chorus "Amen" from _Messiah_ (pp. 89-91)

J. CANTATA (Church Cantata or Lutheran Cantata)

    1. Another large vocal form utilizing arias, recitatives, choruses, and sinfonias

    2. Name implies pieces to be sung (Italian verb _cantare_--to sing)

    3. Used to accompany liturgical services in the Lutheran church

    4. Smaller in scope than an opera or oratorio

    5. Similar in performance style to the oratorio

        a. Not staged or acted

        b. No costumes or scenery

    6. CHORALE

        a. A four-part, homophonic composition

        b. A hymn that is well-known and performed by the entire congregation

        c. Usually the last movement of a cantata

        d. Melodic phrases of the chorale often appear throughout the work

    7. Many examples of church cantatas (almost 300) were composed by J.S. Bach

K. PASSION

    1. A large vocal work that uses arias, recitatives, choruses, and sinfonias

    2. A dramatic sacred work based on the Gospel accounts of the suffering and death of Christ

    3. The most well- known passions are by J.S. Bach:

        a. _The St. Matthew Passion_

        b. _The St. John Passion_

    4. Comparable to the oratorio, yet Bach's style is typically more polyphonic and thick than is Handel's style

L. Of notable interest is J.S. Bach's _Mass in B minor_

    1. Similar in scope to the passions and the oratorios

    2. Not a liturgical work, not intended for a Mass service

    3. A unique, dramatic work that is quite different from the passions and oratorios of other composers

III. Baroque Instrumental Forms (pp. 92-101)

    A. Instrumental skills of Baroque performers was often passed down through family lines

        1. Technical secrets rarely shared outside the family

        2. Master-student relationship was the main source of learning

        3. There were a few method books for amateur performers

    B. The HARPSICHORD

        1. The dominant keyboard instrument in the Baroque

        2. Important for realizing a basso continuo

        3. An essential accompaniment for vocal and instrumental music

        4. In a large ensemble the harpsichordist was also the conductor

        5. The composer was very often the harpsichordist

    C. The TRIO SONATA

        1. A sonata with three instrumental parts

            a. Two treble or high instrumental parts (e.g., violin, oboe, flute)

            b. Basso continuo (bass line)

        2. Results in four players playing three musical lines

    D. The SUITE

        1. A collection of highly stylized dances

        2. Each dance has its own particular rhythmic feature

        3. Intended for listening rather than for dancing (STYLIZED)

        4. First movement was often an introductory piece

            a. Overture

            b. Prelude

        5. Written for various performance media

            a. Large orchestras

            b. Small chamber ensembles

            c. Solo harpsichord or lute

    E. The CONCERTO GROSSO

        1. Genre in which a soloist or small group of soloists are contrasted against a large ensemble

        2. Full orchestra (TUTTI--ALL) plays themes that recur several times (RITORNELLO--RETURN)

        3. Tutti and soloists played themes that were common to both groups and themes that were specific to one group

        4. The concerto grosso is structured around the contrast of the two groups

            a. CONCERTINO

                i. The smaller ensemble

ii. Two or more soloists accompanied by a continuo

    b. TUTTI or RIPIENO

        i. The larger, louder group

        ii. Contrasting volume with the smaller group

    c. TERRACED DYNAMICS

        i. Technique used by Baroque composers to change dynamic levels

        ii. More players were added to the texture or more organ STOPS were used to increase the volume; less players for softer volumes

        iii. Results in sudden rather than gradual dynamic changes

        iv. Good example of Baroque composers' love of contrast

F. ANTONIO VIVALDI (see biography, p. 94)

    1. The most prolific concerto grosso composer of the Baroque

    2. A virtuoso violinist, most of his concerti are for solo or duo violins

    3. Knowledge of instruments allowed for imaginative orchestrations

    4. Instrumental melodies illustrate the intense emotion of the Baroque

    5. An important work is the four solo violin concerti called *The Four Seasons*

        a. Good examples of Vivaldi's control of the Baroque orchestra

        b. Includes short poems in the score before each concerto to help the performers interpret the music

        c. LISTENING NOTES: "Spring," first movement, from *The Four Seasons* (pp. 95-96)

G. ARCANGELO CORELLI

    1. Also an excellent violinist like Vivaldi

    2. Wrote several compositions for the violin

    3. One of the first composers to begin writing concerti for solo violin

    4. Also wrote trio sonatas in two styles

        a. SONATA DA CAMERA (Chamber Sonata)

            i. Similar to the harpsichord suites

            ii. Consists of several dance movements

        b. SONATA DA CHIESA (Church Sonata)

            i. Generally more solemn than the sonata da camera

            ii. Often performed in a church setting before a service

            iii. May include more players per part if room in the church

        c. Corelli's style of trio sonata was widely imitated in Europe in the 18th century

H. JOHANN SEBASTIAN BACH (see biography, pp. 96-97)

    1. One of the most important composers in music history

    2. Equally at home writing vocal or instrumental music

3. The Brandenburg Concertos

    a. Six concertos that exhibit some of the best ensemble writing of the period

    b. Each uses a different group of soloists as the concertino

I. Another important instrument in the Baroque was the pipe organ

    1. Found in cathedrals, churches, and courts all over Europe

    2. Bach was famous in his lifetime as an organist rather than a composer

J. The FUGUE

    1. An important type of composition in an imitative texture

    2. Often preceded by an introductory piece that set the mood for the fugue

        a. PRELUDE

        b. TOCCATA

    3. The parts of the fugue are

        a. The SUBJECT or theme

            i. Stated by the first voice alone

            ii. Theme is repeated by other voices in turn (ANSWER)

            iii. Dramatic texture of the fugue results from the overlapping statements of the subjects and answers

        b. Subject may be accompanied by a COUNTERSUBJECT

            i. A complementary melody played in duet fashion with the answer

            ii. Intensifies the texture of the fugue

        c. Different sections of the fugue that featured the subject were separated by free melodic sections called EPISODES

        d. The FINAL CADENCE was often announced by a prolonged, low note in the bass range or pedals of the organ--PEDAL TONE

            i. Announces the upcoming approach of the tonic key

            ii. The dominant chord played over the pedal point increased the tension

    4. LISTENING NOTES: *Fugue in G Minor* ("The Little"; pp. 99-100)

K. The CHORALE PRELUDE

    1. An organ piece based on a Lutheran chorale melody

    2. Often an improvised piece that preceded the singing of the chorale in church

    3. Some examples sound very dissonant and chromatic

IV. French Baroque Composers (p. 101)

A. JEAN-BAPTISTE LULLY

    1. Wrote several opera-ballets that contrasted with the Italian opera styles

    2. Emphasized instrumental dances

    3. Typically very long operas that set the pattern for all French opera

B. JEAN-PHILIPPE RAMEAU

1. Well-known music theorist and philosopher in the18th century

2. Developed a style of French recitative that made it possible to project the dialogue over the orchestra

C. French opera had instrumental and vocal qualities that reflected the influence of Italian vocal styles

EXERCISES

1. Listen to a recording of the first movement of the Brandenburg Concerto No. 2 by Johann Sebastian Bach. Listen closely to determine the instruments that make up the small group of soloists called the CONCERTINO. Devise a graphic map that shows how this concerto movement is constructed. By using different colored pencils or pens it is very easy to distinguish the solo instruments of the concertino both from each other and from the instruments of the full orchestra or TUTTI. Map out in your graph at what points in the movement the tutti plays and at what points the soloists play. The different colors will reveal a textural map to help describe the music. Write up your findings in a brief paper. Be sure to include a key to your map.

2. Compare at least three of the following dance examples. What are the rhythms that define each of these dances? Are all the meters the same? On what beat do the strong accents of each dance type occur? In what way do these accents define the dance movement? For each dance that you examine, make a graph of the dance rhythms by using long and short lines to indicate note lengths. Show where barlines are and where the strong accents are in relation to the barlines. Write up our findings in a brief essay. **NOTE:** Menuett I and II and Gavotte I and II each count as one dance example.

    Bach: Orchestral Suite No. 1--Courante, Menuett I and II

    Orchestral Suite No. 2--Sarabande, Polonaise

    Orchestral Suite No. 3--Gavotte I and II, Bourée, Gigue

3. Listen to a few examples of arias and recitatives from *The Beggar's Opera* by John Gay and compare these to some examples taken from *Giulio Cesare* by George Frideric Handel. Examine the storylines and characters of each work. How do you think these works would have been accepted in 18th century, middle-class London society? Would one be more accepted than the other? Why? Do you think the audience of that time would relate better to one opera than to the other? Is your opinion based on more than just the differences in language?

1. The emphasis on detail is the essence of the Baroque period. (p. 82)

    A. True

    B. False

2. The music of the Baroque focuses on an increased expression of _Emotion_ and a love of _Contrast_. (p 82)

3. A new solo vocal style developed in the Baroque is called (p. 82)

    A. Madrigal

    B. Monody

    C. Monophony

    D. Motet

4. This style of vocal music was developed by the _Florintine_ _Camarata_ (p. 82)

5. The declamatory vocal style above a prominent bass and used to relate a text is called (p. 82)

    A. Recitative

    B. Figured bass

    C. Monophony

    D. Aria

6. The practice of writing numbers below the bass line to indicate the intervals to be played above the bass is called _Figured_ bass. (pp. 82-83)

7. Another name for thorough bass is _Basso Continuo_. (p. 82)

8. A repeated melody in the bass that supports the melodies above it is called (p. 83)

    A. Basso obligatto

    B. Basso ostinato

    C. Basso a cappella

    D. Basso orchestrato

9. Another name for the bass line named above is _Ground Bass_. (p. 83)

10. The bass line became less important throughout the Baroque period. (p. 83)

    A. True

    B. False

11. The major vocal form that developed in the Baroque period was _Opera_. (p. 83)

12. The first opera house opened in 1637 in (p. 83)

    A. Vienna

    B. Vincennes

    C. Venice

    D. Versailles

13. The instrumental musical sections in early opera were called _Sinfonias_. (p. 83)

14. Why were these instrumental musical sections used in early opera? (p. 83)

    to add contrast to vocal sections

15. One of the important developers of early Italian opera was (p. 84)

    A. Claudio Monteverdi

    B. Giovanni Gabrieli

    C. Antonio Vivaldi

    D. George Frideric Handel

16. The lyric song used in opera, oratorios, and cantatas is (p. 84)

    A. Recitative

    B. Aria

    C. Monody

    D. Bel canto

17. A _Virtuoso_ is a musician who excels above all others and is a superior musician. (p. 84)

18. The singing style which emphasized vocal technique and display is known as (p. 84)

    A. Recitative

    B. Aria

    C. Monody

    D. Bel canto

19. The type of song that is most popular for these virtuosic displays is known as _Da Capo_ aria. (p. 84)

20. The form of the aria named above is (p. 84)

    A. Binary

    B. Theme and variations

    C. Ternary

    D. Rondo

21. A vocal style that is accompanied only by the continuo is _Dry_ recitative. (p. 85)

22. The section of an opera, cantata, or oratorio that is performed with several singers on a part is (p. 85)

    A. The chorale

    B. The aria

    C. The recitative

    D. The chorus

23. Male singers who sang soprano and alto roles in early opera were called _Castriti_. (p. 86)

24. Why are recitatives and arias evenly balanced in early operas? (p. 86)

    provide contrast & drama to opera

56

Identify each of the following characteristics with the aria or with the recitative. Mark "A" (aria) or "R" (recitative) in the space provided. (p. 87)

25. __A__ Expressive, flowing melody

26. __A__ Full orchestral accompaniment

27. __R__ No regular strong meter

28. __A__ Usually embellished by the singer

29. __R__ Usually accompanied by the continuo only

30. __A__ Repetitive rhythms

31. __A__ Large vocal and instrumental range used to intensify the texture

32. __R__ The flow of the notes and the level of activity are governed by the text

33. __A__ Displays vocal intensity and emotion

34. __R__ Melody is descriptive and speech-like

35. A new style of opera that appealed to the middle class is _Ballad_ opera. (p. 87)

36. Which of the following is NOT true of ballad opera (p. 87)

    (A.) Was much larger in scope than traditional opera

    B. Usually has humorous or light plots

    C. Uses familiar melodies

    D. Led to a decline in serious opera

37. The most significant composer in England in the 1720s was (p. 87)

    A. Johann Sebastian Bach

    B. Henry Purcell

    (C.) George Frideric Handel

    D. Antonio Vivaldi

38. A large vocal work similar to opera and based on a sacred subject is called _Oratorio_. (p.87)

39. The vocal form named above was more expensive to produce than opera was. (p. 87)

    A. True

    (B.) False

40. Which of the following is the main difference between opera and oratorio? (pp. 87-88)

    A. The use of arias and recitatives

    (B.) The subject matter of stories

    C. The use of orchestra for accompaniment

    D. The inclusion of sinfonias

41. Oratorios were not usually staged or costumed. (p. 87)

    (A.) True

    B. False

42. For what reason might a chorus be used more often in an oratorio than a solo voice? (pp. 88-89)

Express noble & sacred feelings

43. The texture of a chorus is usually more polyphonic than an aria. (p. 89)

   A. True

   B. False

44. Handel did not write Italian operas. (p. 91)

   A. True

   B. False

45. The large vocal form with arias, recitatives, and choruses that accompanied the liturgical Lutheran calendar is called a _Cantata_. (p. 91)

46. The Lutheran hymn typically sung as the last movement to the large vocal form named above is called (p. 91)

   A. A chorale

   B. An aria

   C. A recitative

   D. A chorus

47. A dramatic sacred work similar to the oratorio but specifically characterizes the suffering and death of Christ is known as a _Passion_. (p.92)

48. Bach's Mass in B Minor was not meant to be a liturgical work. (p. 92)

   A. True

   B. False

49. Instrumental skills in the Baroque were usually learned in special schools. (p. 92)

   A. True

   B. False

50. The dominant keyboard instrument in the Baroque was (p. 92)

   A. The piano

   B. The clavichord

   C. The harpsichord

   D. The lute

51. The musical director for chamber groups, orchestras, and operas usually played (p. 92)

   A. The flute

   B. The first violin

   C. The harpsichord

   D. The lute

52. The bass line of the continuo part was usually reinforced with a _cello_. (p. 92)

53. The number of instrumentalists in a Baroque trio sonata is _4_. (p. 92)

54. In a trio sonata, the two upper parts are performed by soloists. (p. 92)

    A. *(circled)* True

    B. False

55. An instrumental collection of dances is called a _Suite_. (p. 93)

56. All the movements of the instrumental form named above are dances. (p. 93)

    A. True

    B. *(circled)* False

57. Rhythmic characteristics of dance forms were derived from _Dace Steps_. (p. 93)

58. Name two media that performed these instrumental dance collections. (p. 93)

    A. _Orchestras_

    B. _Solo Instruments_

59. An instrumental form which contrasts a soloist or group of soloists against a larger orchestra
    is called a _Concert gross_. (p. 93)

60. The large orchestra in the form named above is called the _tutti_ or _Ritornello_.
    (p. 93)

61. The most prolific composer of this instrumental form in the 18th century was (pp. 93-94)

    A. Johann Sebastian Bach

    B. Henry Purcell

    C. George Frideric Handel

    D. *(circled)* Antonio Vivaldi

62. The group of soloists in the instrumental named above is called (p. 94)

    A. The ritornello

    B. *(circled)* The concertino

    C. The ripieno

    D. The tutti

63. The sudden change in dynamic levels between the solo group and the full orchestra is
    called _Terraced dynamics_ (p. 94)

64. The levers on an organ that are used to open up more pipes are called _Stops_. (p. 94)

65. One of the first composers to write concerti specifically for string instruments was (p. 97)

    A. Claudio Monteverdi

    B. John Gay

    C. *(circled)* Arcangelo Corelli

    D. George Frideric Handel

66. The type of Baroque sonata that was based on dance forms is the sonata _Da Camera_ (p. 97)

67. The type of sonata that was performed in a church setting is the sonata _Da Chiesa_ (p. 97)

68. These styles of sonata were widely imitated in the 18th century. (p. 97)

A. True

B. False

69. Which of the following are parts of a fugue? (pp. 98-99)

A. Exposition and gigue

B. Subject and recitative

C. Countersubject and chorale

D. Subject and countersubject

70. Fugues are often preceded by *Prelude* or *toccata*. (p. 98)

71. The main theme of a fugue is called the *Subject*. (p. 99)

72. The above named theme is sometimes accompanied in duet fashion by (p. 99)

A. The subject

B. The pedal point

C. The countersubject

D. The toccata

73. A long, low note near the end of a fugue that announces the final tonic destination is called (p. 99)

A. The subject

B. The pedal point

C. The countersubject

D. The toccata

74. Statements of the main theme or themes in a fugue are alternated with melodically free material called *Episodes*. (p. 99)

75. An organ work that is based on a Lutheran chorale melody is called a *Chorale Prelude*. (p. 100)

76. The above named organ work was often improvised in church. (p. 100)

A. True

B. False

77. An important composer of opera-ballet was (p. 101)

A. Jean-Baptiste Lully

B. Henry Purcell

C. Johann Sebastian Bach

D. Henri Rousseau

78. An important French opera composer, theorist, and philosopher was *Jean Phillipe Rameau* (p. 101)

79. The main difference, besides language, that differentiates French and Italian opera is the French emphasis on *instrumenta dances for Ballet*. (p. 101)

60

CHAPTER 8, THE VIENNESE PERIOD: 1750 to 1830

In Chapter 8, the author discusses the music of what is one of the most recognizable periods in Western European music history--the Viennese Classical Period. The composers who were active at this time--Haydn, Mozart, and Beethoven--are perhaps the most well-known composers of all time. These composers, and others who are less well-known, are responsible for developing several musical forms and musical genres that are still in use today. The important genres or types of music that are discussed in this chapter are the SYMPHONY, the STRING QUARTET, the SOLO CONCERTO, and the SOLO SONATA. These are all instrumental forms. In vocal music important developments occurred in opera in the hands of Mozart and his predecessor, Christoph Gluck. The Classical forms that were developed and/or used extensively in this period include SONATA-ALLEGRO form, MINUET AND TRIO, RONDO, and THEME AND VARIATIONS.

The music of the Classical period shows a marked difference from that of the Baroque period. The texture is predominantly HOMOPHONIC rather than imitative polyphony; there is more use of gradually changing dynamics rather than the Baroque terraced dynamics; melodies are graceful and symmetrical rather than long, drawn-out, and heavily ornate; and there is less active harmonic structures rather than the complex harmonic changes of the Baroque.   The orchestra increases in size in the Classical Period and composers discontinue the use of the Baroque basso continuo.

I. Musical Expansion and Line (pp. 103-104)

    A.   The ROCOCO or GALANT STYLE (c. 1715-1740)

        1.   Reaction against complex imitative polyphony of the Baroque

        2.   Move toward thinning the musical texture

        3.   A transitional period between the Baroque and the mature Viennese Classical style

    B.   Visual and literary artists imitated the cultural examples of ancient Greece and Rome

    C.   Classical composers developed an interpretation of "classical" in regards to music

        1.   Smooth melodic lines made of small MOTIVES

            a.   Short rhythmic or melodic fragments with an identifiable character

            b.   Offer many possibilities of development

            c.   The building blocks for THEMES and THEME GROUPS

        2.   Motivic development became the main technique in expanding the symphony

        3.   Accompaniment was used to enhance the melody

II. The Symphony (p. 104)

    A.   A large, four-movement work for orchestra

    B.   Developed from Baroque instrumental suites and sonatas

    C.   Designed to support extensive thematic or motivic development

III. Four-Movement Works (pp. 104-105)

    A. The STRING QUARTET

        1. Musical group comprised of two violins, a viola, and a cello

        2. The chamber music equivalent of the symphony

        3. LISTENING NOTES: Haydn, *String Quartet in E-flat, Op. 33, No. 2* ("The Joke"; Topic 6, pp. 264-265)

        4. LISTENING NOTES: Beethoven, *String Quartet in C-sharp Minor, Op. 131* (Topic 6, pp. 266-267)

    B. Both symphony and quartet consist of four movements

        1. Third movement (minuet and trio) is the only movement that retained dance characteristics

        2. Other movements were forms that were developed in the period

            a. SONATA-ALLEGRO

                i. A large form used for the first movement of a symphony or quartet

                ii. Themes are exposed, developed, and recapitulated

            b. RONDO

                i. Form often used as the last movement of a multi-movement work

                ii. First theme is restated between a series of new themes

            c. THEME AND VARIATIONS

                i. A form that may appear as a single work or as a movement in a larger work

                ii. Melodic theme is stated and then varied almost to the point of obscurity

            d. See Chapter 4 for diagrams

IV. The Sonata-Allegro Form (pp. 105-112)

    A. The most important form developed in the Classical period

    B. Consists of three sections each with its own dramatic purpose

        1. EXPOSITION (first section)

            a. Presents first or primary theme in the tonic key

            b. Presents second theme or theme groups in a related key

                i. Dominant key

                ii. Relative major (if tonic key is in the minor mode)

        2. DEVELOPMENT (second section)

            a. Develops first and second themes or theme groups

                i. Frequent modulation away from the tonic

                ii. Themes are often broken down into smaller units

            b. Very unstable harmonically, creates much tension

3. RECAPITULATION (third section)

    a. Restates the material of the exposition

    b. All themes or theme groups REMAIN IN THE TONIC KEY

    c. Resolves the tension of the unstable development

C. Dramatic possibilities of repetition and contrast have inspired imaginative composers

D. DIVERTIMENTI (DIVERSIONS or ENTERTAINMENTS)

    1. A collection of short, dance-like forms

    2. Predecessors to the string quartet

    3. One of the genres that led to the development of sonata-allegro form

        a. Middle section (development) gradually became more important

        b. Early developments were short section of motivic activity to contrast with the more stable exposition and recapitulation

        c. Expanded in the hands of Haydn to become the equal of the other two sections

E. Sonata-allegro form presented a new idea of tonal stability

    1. Each section is identified by key areas and themes

        a. Exposition

            i. First theme: tonic key

            ii. Second theme or theme group: dominant (or relative major)

        b. Development increase tension by departing farther from the tonic

        c. Recapitulation stabilizes the movement by restating all themes in the tonic

    2. Key is an organizational parameter

    3. Resolution of key is the main goal for many large works

F. FRANZ JOSEPH HAYDN (see biography, pp. 106-107)

    1. One of the major composers of the Viennese Classical style

    2. Important figure in the early development of the string quartet and the symphony

    3. LISTENING NOTES: *Symphony 94 in G Major*, movements I and II("Surprise"; pp. 107-109)

G. The Classical symphony developed quickly

    1. Haydn was responsible for much early development

    2. Mozart continued developing the symphonic genre

    3. Beethoven expanded the symphony beyond the scope of the Classical period

    4. The symphony became the dominant form for early Romantic composers

    5. LISTENING EXAMPLE: Beethoven, *Symphony 5 in C Minor, Op. 67* (Topic 2, pp. 220-222)

H. LUDWIG VAN BEETHOVEN (see biography, p. 111)

    1. One of the most important composers in music history

2. Excellent piano performer with great improvisational skills

3. Mature compositions expanded earlier forms

    a. One movement of the 3rd Symphony is longer than a complete Haydn symphony

    b. Expanded the development process in the symphony

    c. Development of themes was expanded in development sections

    d. Further thematic development was present in CODAS and TRANSITIONS

        i. Coda

           1. Extension at the end of a movement

           2. May be very long or very short

        ii. Transition

           1. Occur between themes or theme groups

           2. May introduce new material

           3. Used to modulate to new key areas

4. Beethoven had a broad musical background which led to his composing for diverse instrumental and vocal combinations

5. Eventually became (perhaps the first) "freelance" composer

    a. Performed and conducted his own works

    b. Eventually gave up performing due to increasing deafness

    c. Continued to make a good living composing and publishing music

V. Soloistic Three-Movement Works (p. 112)

  A. Three-movement Classical works usually involved soloists

  B. Resulted primarily from the elimination of third movement Minuet and Trio from four-movement works

    1. First movement uses sonata-allegro form

    2. Second movement is slow, provides rest after first movement

    3. Third movement returns to fast tempo

  C. The SOLO CONCERTO

    1. Features an instrumental soloist and large orchestra

    2. Many solo concerti were written for the new pianoforte

    3. A showcase for technically brilliant performers

    4. Important feature of the concerto is the CADENZA

        a. Short section for solo, unaccompanied improvisation

        b. Rhythmically free in tempo, pulse, and meter

    5. Composers often performed the solo parts of their own concerti

    6. LISTENING NOTES: Haydn, *Trumpet Concerto in E-flat Major*, movement III (Topic 5, pp. 253-254)

D. The SOLO SONATA

    1. "Sonata" was originally a term used to describe instrumental music

    2. In the Classical period, a piece for a solo performer or a soloist with piano accompaniment

    3. Late in the period, the piano accompaniment became more equal to the soloist

    4. LISTENING NOTES: Beethoven, *Piano Sonata in F Minor, Op. 57* ("Appassionata"; Topic 5, pp. 261-262)

VI. Vocal Music (p. 113)

A. Sacred vocal works (Masses, oratorios) continued to be composed in Vienna

B. Haydn continued the oratorio tradition of Handel

    1. *The Creation*

    2. *The Seasons*

C. Mozart's *Requiem* (Mass for the Dead) illustrates the possibilities of serious, weighty writing in the Classical period

D. Several great changes take place in OPERA

VII. Opera (pp. 113-118)

A. REFORM OPERA

    1. A form of serious opera with more balance between music and drama

    2. Blends music, drama, and dance into a theatrical whole

    3. Less contrast between aria and recitative

    4. Aria and recitative have more dramatic moments

    5. Reform movement initiated by CHRISTOPH WILLIBALD GLUCK

    6. EXAMPLE: Gluck, *Orfeo ed Euridice*

        a. Gluck successfully set French language to music

        b. Established the OVERTURE as an important part of the opera

        c. Used the orchestra to establish and identify themes

        d. A general move to simplicity in melody and texture

B. COMIC OPERAS

    1. Very popular form of opera in England, Italy, and Germany

    2. Not part of the serious opera tradition

    3. Each country had a special name for comic opera

        a. France: OPÉRA COMIQUE

            i. Based on satire

            ii. Developed into a more realistic form in the late 19th century

        b. Germany: SINGSPIEL

            i. Based on folk tales

            ii. Uses spoken dialogue instead of recitative

     c.   Italy: OPERA BUFFA

         i.   Generally placed characters in socially humorous situations

         ii. Uses recitative rather than spoken dialogue

         iii. Usually ends with an ENSEMBLE FINALE

            1. Several singers perform at the same time but different melodies and different texts

            2. Creates a clever, complex web of polyphony

     d.   All forms of comic opera used folk songs and popular songs

D. WOLFGANG AMADEUS MOZART (see biography, p. 114)

    1. One of the major composers in music history

    2. Composed in all forms and genres popular in the Classical period

    3. Mozart's operas clearly exhibit his skill in setting words to music and his understanding of human psychology

       a.   Enhanced the drama by controlling key areas

       b.   Drama also supported by Mozart's manipulation of themes

       c.   Uses large forms in his operas that are equal in stature to the instrumental forms being developed in this period

    4. LISTENING NOTES: *Le nozze di Figaro (The Marriage of Figaro)*, excerpts from Act I (pp. 116-118)

VIII. Patronage and the Working Musician (pp. 118-119)

A. The social environment of the Classical period created a patronage system among the aristocracy to hire composers and performers

B. Musicians were basically hired help or servants

C. Gradually other sources of income for composers were developed

    1. Music publishing became a substantial business

    2. Public concerts were increasingly popular with the rising middle class

    3. Composers became increasingly independent of their aristocratic patrons

D. Haydn

    1. Employed for over thirty years by the Esterhazy family

    2. Gradually became independent of sole patronage

E. Mozart

    1. Caught between the "menial labor" of the patronage system and the idea of the independent, self-supporting musician

    2. Performed and composed just to make a living, but died in poverty

    3. Could not solicit patrons to subsidize his works

F. Beethoven

    1. Broke away from the image of the musician as servant

    2. Received his greatest support from the concert-going middle class

    3. Continued to nurture relationships with the aristocracy

    4. Demonstrated great skill in balancing patronage, publication, and performance

    5. The music industry after Beethoven gave increasing support to struggling composers

EXERCISES

1. Listen to the first movements of at least two of the following piano sonatas. Consider how the composers deal with form, melody, and harmony in each example. Each of these movements is in sonata-allegro form. In what way or ways does each composer remain true to the form as has been discussed in the text? In what ways have the composers taken liberties with the form in the interest of artistic freedom? Is the form fairly clear to hear or is it disguised? How are transitional sections used? Are any of these examples melodically similar to each other? Are they melodically very different from one another? Is there anything else that attracts your attention?

Haydn	Mozart	Beethoven
Sonata No. 20 in C minor	Sonata in C minor, K. 457	Sonata No. 1 in F minor, Op. 2, No. 1
		Sonata No. 8 in C minor, Op. 13

2. Listen to the aria "Madamina! Il catalogo è questo" from the opera *Don Giovanni* by Mozart. Pay close attention to the words with a translation of the LIBRETTO (translations of the libretto are included with recordings). In a brief essay, describe the meaning of the words and then relate how Mozart's music, both the orchestral accompaniment and the principal vocal line, is used to enhance the meaning of the words.

3. Listen to the symphony movements listed below. Describe how each composer uses sonata-allegro form as the basis of each movement. Include in your discussion the ways in which each composer uses various musical elements to help define sections of the movements. Some elements you may want to include are TEXTURE, HARMONY and MODULATION, RHYTHM, INSTRUMENTATION and ORCHESTRATION, MELODIC SHAPE, TEMPO, and DYNAMICS. Do you find that these symphony movements are similar or are they quite different?

Haydn: Symphony No. 104 in D Major ("London"), 1st movement

Mozart: Symphony No. 41 in C Major ("Jupiter"), 4th movement

Beethoven: Symphony No. 3 in E-flat Major ("Eroica"), 1st movement

1. The artistic style that served as a transition from the Baroque to the Classical periods was (p. 103)

    A.   The Viennese

    B.   The Cartesian

    C.   The Rococo

    D.   The Brocade

2. Another name for this transitional style period is the ___galant___ style. (p. 103)

3. What brought about this transitional style period? (p. 103)

    _____

4. The art of this transitional period is often referred to as light and frivolous. (p. 103)

    A.   True

    B.   False

5. The city that became the center of activity in the Classical period is _____. (p. 103)

6. Why is the time period from c. 1750 to c. 1830 known as the Classical period? (p. 103)

    _____

7. A small musical unit that is made of a short identifiable rhythm and a few pitches is called (p. 103)

    A.   A phrase

    B.   A theme

    C.   A theme group

    D.   A motive

8. These small musical units are the basis or building blocks of unique melodies called (p. 103)

    A.   A phrase

    B.   A theme

    C.   A theme group

    D.   A motive

9. The principal technique in expanding the symphony is ___Motivic   development___
    (p. 103)

10. From what genres of the Baroque period did the symphony develop? (p. 104)

    A.   _____

    B.   _____

11. The chamber music equivalent of the symphony is (p. 104)

    A.   The solo sonata

    B.   The trio sonata

    C.   The string quartet

    D.   The solo concerto

12. The genre named in question 11 and the symphony typically have how many movements? (p. 104)

    A.   Four

    B.   Two

    C.   Three

    D.   Five

13. The only movement that retained a connection with the dance suite was the __third__

    _____ _____. (pp. 104-105)

14. The principal large form that was used for the first movement of a symphony is _____

    _____ form. (p. 105)

15. The three sections that make up this form are the _____, the _____,

    and the _____. (p. 105)

16. The first theme in the first section is in which key? (p. 105)

    A.   Dominant

    B.   Subdominant

    C.   Tonic

    D.   Secondary dominant

17. The second theme or theme group in the first section is in which key? (p. 105)

    A.   Dominant

    B.   Subdominant

    C.   Tonic

    D.   Secondary dominant

18. In the second section of this form, themes are broken down and subjected to heavy

    _____ or key change. (p. 105)

19. What is the primary difference between the first section of this form and the second section? (p. 105)

    _____

20. The formal structure in which a principal theme is restated between a series of new themes

    is called _____ form. (p. 105)

21. A collection of dance-like movements performed by small string ensembles is called (p. 105)

    A.   A sonata

    B.   A divertimento

    C.   Theme and variations

    D.   A development

22. One of the first major composers of the new Classical style was _____. (p. 106)

23. The Hungarian noble family for whom the above named composer worked for over thirty

    years is the _____ family. (p. 106)

24. The organizational parameter of many large works is _____ _____. (p. 109)

25. The composer who expanded the symphony beyond the scope of the Classical period is (p. 109)

   A.   Salieri

   B.   Haydn

   C.   Mozart

   D.   Beethoven

26. The musical extension at the end of a movement is called (p. 110)

   A.   A conduct

   B.   A coda

   C.   A consequence

   D.   A cadenza

27. The sections that appear between themes or theme groups and help introduce new material

   are _____ sections. (p. 110)

28. The above named sections can be developmental in nature and are characterized by (p. 110):

   A.   _____

   B.   _____

29. Why did Beethoven have to give up performing? (p. 112)

   _____

30. How did Beethoven make a living after he gave up performing? (p. 112)

   _____

31. Beethoven was one of the first full-time "freelance" composers. (p. 112)

   A.   True

   B.   False

32. The three movement works that developed in the Classical period usually involved

   _____. (p. 112)

33. The typical tempos of the three movement works were slow, fast, fastest. (p. 112)

   A.   True

   B.   False

34. The three movement work that featured the contrast of a soloist against a full orchestra is (p. 112)

   A.   Solo sonata

   B.   Solo sinfonia

   C.   Solo concerto

   D.   Solo divertimento

35. In most of the above named works in the Classical period, the solo instrument was the

   harpsichord. (p. 112)

   A.   True

   B.   False

36. The short section of a concerto movement where the orchestra stops and the soloist improvises is called (p. 112)

    A.   A conduct

    B.   A coda

    C.   A consequence

    D.   A cadenza

37. The three movement work that is played by a solo instrument or a solo instrument accompanied by a piano is called (p. 112)

    A.   Solo sonata

    B.   Solo sinfonia

    C.   Solo concerto

    D.   Solo divertimento

38. The traditional large, sacred vocal works of the Classical period were _____ and _____. (p. 113)

39. The composer who is credited with reforming opera in the 18th century is (p. 113)

    A.   Mozart

    B.   Gluck

    C.   Haydn

    D.   Beethoven

40. In the operas of the above named composer the contrast between the recitative and aria was softened in order to better support the dramatic moments. (p. 113)

    A.   True

    B.   False

41. Name two ways in which the composer in question 39 above accomplished opera reform. (p. 113)

    A.   _____

    B.   _____

42. The text of an opera that is designed to be set to music is called the _____. (p. 113)

43. The French form of comic opera is called _____ _____. (p. 113)

44. The German form of comic opera is called _____. (p. 113)

45. The Italian form of comic opera is called _____ _____. (p. 115)

46. A characteristic of the German type of comic opera is (p. 113)

    A.   There is no orchestra

    B.   The stories are based on Greek mythology

    C.   There are no solo arias

    D.   The stories are based on folk tales

47. The Italian type of comic opera usually ended with _____ _____. (p. 115)

48. All of these comic opera forms relied on spoken dialogue instead of recitative. (p. 115)

   A.   True

   B.   False

49. In what ways did Mozart enhance the drama of his operas? (p. 115)

   A.   _____

   B.   _____

50. The structures of Mozart's operas are not on the same level as the structures of his
    instrumental works. (p. 115)

   A.   True

   B.   False

51. The system in which composers worked for a wealthy or noble family and produced music
    for the entertainment of these families and their friends is called _____. (p.118)

52. Name two other ways a composer could make a living in music besides working within
    the above named system. (p. 118)

   A.   _____

   B.   _____

53. Which composer had trouble soliciting wealthy people to support his music? (p. 118)

   A.   Mozart

   B.   Schubert

   C.   Haydn

   D.   Beethoven

54. Which composer broke away from the old system and received his greatest support from
    the middle class? (p. 119)

   A.   Mozart

   B.   Schubert

   C.   Haydn

   D.   Beethoven

55. Which composer worked well within the old system and worked for the same family for
    over 30 years? (p. 118)

   A.   Mozart

   B.   Schubert

   C.   Haydn

   D.   Beethoven

CHAPTER 9, THE ROMANTIC PERIOD: 1830 to 1900

This chapter deals with the composers and the music of the 19th century, what has become known as the Romantic Period in music history. The composers of this era for the most part followed the lead that was established by Beethoven in the first quarter of the century. As in Beethoven's works, symphonies increased in both length and scope. There was a wider range of dynamic levels from very soft to very loud, and tempos were varied dramatically within single movements. Another important change is seen in the growth of the orchestra. Several new instruments were added to the orchestra and some established instrumental sections, such as the horns, were greatly expanded in size. Composers experimented with new combinations of instruments and colorful, dissonant harmonies came to be used for expression. The first textbooks on orchestration were written in the 19th century.

There was a new attitude in expression in the 19th century. Composers shifted from the idea of creating a well-crafted piece of music, as in the Classical Period, to expressing personal emotions in their art. Emotion took the place of logic in the arts. Two favorite topics for operas and instrumental music in the 19th century were NATIONALISM and EXOTICISM. New means of expression were developed from the very small and intimate MINIATURES and ART SONGS to the large symphonies and grandiose operas. Program music grew as composers used instrumental forms, such as symphonies or the newly developed SYMPHONIC POEM, to convey extra-musical ideas. Programmatic symphonies were written to describe paintings, poems, natural objects such as rivers and sea coasts, and other non-musical ideas through music alone.

I. The Art Song (pp. 121-126)

    A. Solo compositions are perhaps the most representative forms of expression in the Romantic period

    B. Words were given added emotional significance by way of the instrumental accompaniment

    C. The piano accompanist became of equal importance with the soloist

    D. Every country had a form of ART SONG or LIED (in German)

        1. Written for singing at home or in another intimate setting

        2. Texts cover many topics, but romance is the most common

        3. Considered a type of MINIATURE

        4. Composers turned to the long tradition of word painting to help describe the text

    E. Songs were often grouped into SONG CYCLES

        1. A series of poems based on related themes set to music

        2. When viewed as a whole, song cycles are larger works

        3. Groups of two or three songs may be used to balance another group of songs

        4. The overall structure of a song cycle may be a large binary or ternary form

F. Structure of single songs fall into two categories

    1. STROPHIC

        a. Several verses or poem stanzas set to the same music

        b. Provides a system of repetition that audiences can understand

        c. Generally easier to remember and became audience favorites

        d. The most familiar song form

    2. THROUGH-COMPOSED (from German *durchkomponiert*)

        a. Songs without repeated sections of music

        b. Very dramatic format of song

        c. Story unfolds and characters change moods as the music changes

        d. The music amplifies the story line

        e. Even though the poetic text may be strophic, the music will change from stanza to stanza, resulting in the through-composed form

G. FRANZ SCHUBERT (see biography, pp. 122-123)

    1. A Viennese composer who composed in most genres of the time

    2. Especially partial to the art song and the song cycle

    3. Considered to have brought the art song to a new level of intensity that was representative of the Romantic idea of expression

    4. LISTENING NOTES: *Gretchen am Spinnrade* (p. 124)

    5. LISTENING NOTES: *Erlkönig* (pp. 125-126)

II. Solo Piano (pp. 126-129)

A. The dominant solo instrument in the 19th century

    1. Named for its ability to play soft (piano) and loud (forte): PIANOFORTE

    2. In the late 18th century, the piano replaced the harpsichord

    3. Offers greater scope of expression than any other instrument except the organ

    4. The piano was well-suited to the expressive needs of the Romantic composer

B. Several types of piano MINIATURES or CHARACTER PIECES were developed by Romantic composers

    1. The pianistic equivalent of the art song

    2. Single-movement forms that are dominated by mood development

    3. Several different types of piano miniatures were written in the 19th century (see chart, pp. 126-127)

        a. NOCTURNE

        b. ETUDE

        c. POLONAISE

        d. MAZURKA

       e.   IMPROMPTU

       f.   BALLADE

       g.   PRELUDE

   4.   Works of composers like Schumann and Brahms explored the available sonorities of the piano

C.   FRÉDÉRIC CHOPIN (see biography, p. 127)

   1.   One of the major composers of piano music in the 19th century

   2.   Also known for his skill as a performer and improviser on the piano

   3.   Composed examples of all piano miniature forms listed above

   4.   Chopin's works explore the rich harmonies and sonorities available on the piano

   5.   LISTENING NOTES: *Etude in C Minor, Op. 10, No. 12* (p. 128)

III. Program Music (pp. 129-132)

A.   The instrumental equivalent of the emotional and expressive art song

B.   Based on a non-musical idea, usually of a literary type

   1.   Poem

   2.   Story

   3.   Title

   4.   Play

   5.   Painting

   6.   Item in nature, e.g., a river, a mountain, a town

C.   The music is meant to interpret the story or mood of the program

D.   Contrast with ABSOLUTE MUSIC

   1.   Instrumental music with no extraneous program

   2.   Retains generic titles, e.g., symphony, concerto, quartet

   3.   FELIX MENDELSSOHN (see biography, Topic 5, p. 255), LISTENING NOTES: *Violin Concerto in E Minor, Op. 64,* 1st movement (Topic 5, pp. 256-257)

E.   Three basic forms of program music

   1.   CONCERT OVERTURES

       a.   Single-movement works usually in sonata-allegro form

       b.   Concert overture was not intended to precede an opera or play

       c.   The title was used to define the mood of the instrumental drama

       d.   EXAMPLES

          i.   Tchaikovsky, *Romeo and Juliet Overture*

          ii.   Mendelssohn, *Hebrides Overture*

   2.   TONE POEMS or SYMPHONIC POEMS

       a.   Long, single-movement compositions

b.   Commonly used sonata-allegro form or rondo form

c.   Irregular forms were used for unusual or unique stories (through-composed)

d.   EXAMPLES

   i.   R. Strauss, *Don Juan*

   ii.   Dukas, *The Sorcerer's Apprentice*

   iii.   FRANZ LISZT (see biography, Topic 1, p. 211), LISTENING NOTES: *Les Preludes* (Topic 1, pp. 212-213)

3.   PROGRAM SYMPHONIES

a.   Similar to single-movement tone poems but expanded for organization and development

b.   Uses a program to unify a multi-movement work

c.   Each movement typically has a title or phrase as a program

F.   An important composer of program symphonies was HECTOR BERLIOZ (see biography, p. 132)

1.   Enlarged the orchestra with additional brass and percussion

2.   Expanded orchestra meant an expansion of dynamic range

3.   The first composer to use dynamic levels greater than fortissimo and less than pianissimo

4.   Revolutionary orchestrater

a.   Used new instrumental combinations

b.   Grouped instruments in non-traditional settings

c.   Produced some of the most exciting examples of tone color of the time

d.   Used the orchestra as his instrument rather than orchestrating sounds that were played on the piano

e.   Wrote one of the first textbooks on orchestration

5.   Most famous work is *Symphonie Fantastique*

a.   An autobiographical program: *An Episode in the Life of an Artist*

b.   Uses a new thematic device called the *idée fixe* (fixed idea)

   i.   A recurring theme that represents the composer's beloved

   ii.   Appears transformed in each movement of the symphony

c.   The program and the startling orchestrations made a strong impression on the Parisian audience

d.   LISTENING NOTES: *Symphonie Fantastique*, 4th movement, "March to the Scaffold" (pp. 130-131)

IV. Opera: Grandeur and Dissonance (pp. 133-140)

    A. Dramatic plots were dominated by passion and emotion

        1. Love between two individuals was so great that when one died the other died also

        2. Emotions expanded by using mythology for plots

            a. Use of magic and the supernatural

            b. Heroes and villains were "larger than life"

    B. The two most powerful opera composers in the 19th century were Verdi and Wagner

    C. GIUSEPPE VERDI (see biography, pp. 133-134)

        1. Believed that opera must be passionate

        2. Opera should also be interesting and provide entertainment

        3. Composed in a conventional manner with emphasis on melody

        4. Orchestrations became increasingly descriptive to support the melody

        5. Arias and recitatives became more and more similar as his style matured

        6. Great ability for building strong musical characterizations

        7. His operas became the models for Italian opera

            a. Typically ended large sections of the drama with ensembles

            b. Several individuals sing at the same time on stage but do not seem to hear one another

            c. Melodies and text were identified with each character in the ensemble

        8. LISTENING NOTES: *Falstaff*, excerpt from Act III, Scene 2 (pp. 134-136)

    D. RICHARD WAGNER (see biography, p. 138)

        1. Believed he wrote operas that were of a larger scope than traditional opera

        2. Characters were often super beings with problems to match

        3. Referred to his works as MUSIC DRAMAS

            a. These works blended all aspects of music and drama

            b. Wagner wrote his own librettos that were derived from myths and legends

            c. He had control over set designs and all visual aspects of the drama

            d. He also wrote all the music

            e. He had built to his specifications an opera house for the sole purpose of putting on his own music dramas

        4. Opera style was quite different from Verdi's style

            a. There is a continuous musical flow

            b. There is no clear division between the arias and the recitatives

            c. The "unending melody" is the unifying thread of the music dramas

            d. Removed traditional places for applause to keep the musical flow going

            e. Large, symphonic instrumental sections become part of the drama

5. *Der Ring des Nibelungen* (*The Ring of the Nibelung*)

    a. A cycle of four music dramas composed between 1848 and 1874

    b. Based on Germanic mythology, the cycle relates Wagner's philosophical beliefs about society

6. An important innovation was Wagner's use of motives: LEITMOTIFS

    a. Melodic and harmonic motives associated with characters, objects, places thoughts, and emotions

    b. Leitmotifs are the unifying features of Wagner's music dramas

    c. Leitmotifs are developed and transformed as plots or characters change

    d. Leitmotifs can be combined with others to transform a character or idea

    e. Most motivic development is done by the large orchestra

        i. Harmonies are rich and chromatic

        ii. Orchestral accompaniment provides great dissonance and tension

        iii. Orchestra provides descriptive colors

        iv. Large orchestra uses an extremely wide range of dynamics

        v. Orchestra was so large that only the strongest voices could be heard over it

7. LISTENING NOTES: *Götterdämmerung* (*The Twilight of the Gods*), conclusion to Act III (pp. 139-140)

V. Nationalism and the Russian Five (pp. 141-144)

    A. An emphasis on nationalism followed in the wake of the French Revolution and the Napoleonic Wars

        1. A deliberate attempt to define national identity in the arts

        2. Musicians quoted folk songs and folk-like melodies in large instrumental works

        3. Patriotic or national subjects were used for operas and tone poems

        4. Composers wanted to show there traditional heritage through their own music

        5. Can be seen as a reaction against the dominance of Italy, France, and Germany in European music

    B. Countries that contributed nationalist composers include

        1. Norway: Edvard Grieg

        2. Finland: Jean Sibelius

        3. Bohemia

            a. Antonin Dvorák

            b. Bedrich Smetna

        4. Russia: The Five

    C. The Russian Five

        1. Five Russian composers who tried to create a truly Russian musical style

2. All but one member were amateur musicians without traditional music training

    a. Mily Balakirev: Music teacher

    b. César Cui: Journalist

    c. Alexander Borodin: Chemist

    d. Nikolai Rimsky-Korsakov: Naval officer, later music professor

    e. Modest Mussorgsky: Government clerk, civil servant

3. Non-traditional training gave them freedom in composing; roughness and rebellion

4. MODEST MUSSORGSKY (see biography, p. 142)

    a. Considered the most significant composer of the Five

    b. Music typically has a harsh, dissonant sound

    c. Melodies and rhythms are angular and rough

    d. Uses folk and folk-like melodies and rhythms

    e. LISTENING NOTES: *Boris Godunov*, Coronation Scene (pp. 143-144)

EXERCISES

1. Listen to song "Die Forelle" ("The Trout") by Franz Schubert--be sure to have a translation of the text handy. In a brief paper describe the content of the text, what the song is about. How is the vocal melody used to describe the story being told? How does the piano accompaniment contribute to the telling of the story? Is this a STROPHIC song or a THROUGH-COMPOSED song or a combination of the two types? In what other ways can you describe the musical content of the song?

2. Listen to the piano miniatures *Carnaval, Op. 9* by Robert Schumann. Each short piece has a descriptive title that identifies a character that each piece represents. The program of this piece is intended to describe a masked ball that these characters are attending. Does the music portray the personality of the characters named in each title? How does Schumann musically describe these characters? Is there a common unifying thread or musical theme that runs through the work or that keeps returning as a character moves around the party? Write up your findings in a brief paper.

3. Listen to the symphonic poem *A Night on Bald Mountain* by Modest Mussorgsky. Be sure to read the program notes that describe the piece, these are usually included on albums or CDs in the liner notes. How does Mussorgsky use the orchestra to tell his story? Describe the orchestral colors that you hear. How does Mussorgsky use dissonance within the orchestra and in the harmonic structure of the piece? Can you describe the images that the music makes you think of? Are your

images based on what you read in the liner notes or do you imagine other, similar scenes? Do you feel that this piece is an effective example of programmatic music? Why or why not?

4. Listen to the Finale of Act II of *Der Freischütz* by Carl Maria von Weber. This scene is often referred to as "The Wolf's Glen" because it takes place deep in the forest at midnight. The story contains elements of magic and the supernatural, particularly at this point in the opera. At this point, the two characters on stage are making magic bullets with incantations at midnight and the weather turning wild and spooky. Describe how this scene makes you feel. What kind of images do you think of with this music? How does Weber use the orchestra to help create a haunted, supernatural atmosphere? Does this scene seem to be more effective because the characters are speaking rather than singing recitative? Do you think that a recitative style of singing would work better? Why or why not?

STUDY QUESTIONS

1. Perhaps the most representative forms of expressive goals for Romantic artists are (p. 121)
    A.   Programmatic symphonies
    B.   Solo compositions
    C.   Piano concertos
    D.   Music dramas

2. The setting of a poem by an established literary writer is called _____ _____. (p.121)

3. The German term for the above named form is _____. (p. 121)

4. Often the accompanying piano is used to give the words extra emotional significance. (p.121)
    A.   True
    B.   False

5. The piano is never of equal importance to the voice. (p. 121)
    A.   True
    B.   False

6. On what long-standing musical tradition did composers rely when setting words to music? (p. 122)
    _____ _____.

7. Composers would often group several songs together into a larger form called a _____
    _____. (p 122)

8. The songs that a composer grouped together were usually related by (p. 122)

    A. A common tonal center

    B. A common meter

    C. A common story content

    D. A common melodic phrase

9. A major composer of Romantic Lieder was (pp. 122-123)

    A. Frederic Chopin

    B. Hector Berlioz

    C. Franz Liszt

    D. Franz Schubert

10. The structure of single songs falls into what two forms? (p. 123)

    A. _____

    B. _____

11. The song form that is easier for audiences to remember because of repetition is _____

    form. (p. 123)

12. The other type of song form relies on _____ and _____-to

    interpret the story. (p. 123)

13. In the song *Gretchen am Spinnrade*, the piano represents (p. 124)

    A. The spinning wheel

    B. The remembered kiss

    C. Gretchen's lover

    D. The moonlit night

14. Because *Gretchen* uses some verses set to the same music as well as extra verses set to

    new music, the form of the song is referred to as _____ _____ form. (p. 124)

15. The dominant instrument in the 19th century was the violin. (p. 126)

    A. True

    B. False

16. The short works of the Romantic period, such as the art song or single-movement piano

    compositions, are called _____. (p. 126)

17. Single-movement piano compositions are also referred to as _____

    pieces. (p. 126)

18. A slow composition for piano with rich, lyric melodies is (pp. 126-127)

    A. A ballade

    B. An etude

    C. A nocturne

    D. A mazurka

19. A short piano composition that demands a great deal of technique and sounds somewhat free and reflective is (pp. 126-127)

    A.   An impromptu

    B.   A polonaise

    C.   A ballade

    D.   A nocturne

20. A short piano composition that was based on a traditional Polish dance is (pp. 126-127)

    A.   A prelude

    B.   A ballade

    C.   An impromptu

    D.   A mazurka

21. A short piano composition designed to develop specific performance techniques is (pp. 126-127)

    A.   A ballade

    B.   An etude

    C.   A nocturne

    D.   A mazurka

22. The composer who wrote almost strictly for piano was _____. (p. 126)

23. The rhythmic device in which the pianist's right hand plays with some freedom against a steady regular rhythm in the left hand is known as _____. (p. 128)

24. Instrumental music which is based on a literary format and is meant to interpret a story is called (p. 129)

    A.   Absolute music

    B.   Miniatures

    C.   Song cycles

    D.   Program music

25. Instrumental music that has no association with literature is called (p. 129)

    A.   Absolute music

    B.   Miniatures

    C.   Song cycles

    D.   Program music

26. The three basic forms of instrumental music named in question 24 above are _____ _____, _____ _____, and _____ _____. (p. 129)

27. A long, single movement composition for orchestra based on a story or poem is (p. 129)

    A.   A song cycle

    B.   A tone poem

    C.   An absolute symphony

    D.   A program symphony

28. The formal structures used most often in the genre named in question 27 are _____

and _____. (p. 129)

29. The genre that is similar to that named in question 27 above, but expanded to include multiple

movements is (p. 129)

   A.   A song cycle

   B.   A tone poem

   C.   An absolute symphony

   D.   A program symphony

30. In the above named genre, only the first movement has a descriptive title. (p. 129)

   A.   True

   B.   False

31. In the *Symphonie fantastique*, Berlioz uses a recurring theme called _____ _____. (p. 130)

32. The above named thematic device appears in altered forms in each movement of the work. (p. 130)

   A.   True

   B.   False

33. The practice of changing a recurring theme to represent a different character of personality

is called _____ _____. (p. 130)

34. What of Berlioz's *Symphonie fantastique* made a strong impression on the Parisians? (p. 131)

   A.   _____

   B.   _____

35. What effect did Berlioz's use of more brass and percussion have on the orchestra? (p. 131)

36. Berlioz was considered a revolutionary because of his instrumental combinations. (p. 131)

   A.   True

   B.   False

37. Another term for the technique of combining instruments or assigning instruments to specific

parts is called _____. (p. 131)

38. Berlioz typically orchestrated what he played on the piano. (p. 131)

   A.   True

   B.   False

39. The two elements that dominated 19th century dramatic works were _____ and

_____. (p. 133)

40. Name two dramatic benefits that the use of mythology lends to opera. (p. 133)

   A.   _____

   B.   _____

41. Verdi believed that opera should be _____ above all else and provide entertainment

for the mass public. (pp. 133-134)

42. Verdi composed in a conventional manner and placed great emphasis on (p. 134)

    A.　Orchestral accompaniment

    B.　Melody

    C.　Strict meters

    D.　Rhythm

43. In order to better support the melody, Verdi's orchestrations became increasingly (p. 134)

    A.　Descriptive

    B.　Thinner

    C.　Abstract

    D.　Atonal

44. As Verdi matured his arias and recitatives became more and more similar. (p. 134)

    A.　True

    B.　False

45. What musical quality set Verdi apart from his contemporaries? (p. 134)

    _____

46. Wagner called his operatic works _____ _____. (p. 136)

47. Why did Wagner refer to his operatic works by this name? (p. 136)

    _____

48. From what sources did Wagner often draw for his librettos? (p. 136)

    A.　_____

    B.　_____

49. Wagner wrote the music and his partner wrote the libretto. (p. 136)

    A.　True

    B.　False

50. An opera house was built to Wagner's specifications in order to have a place to perform his works. (p. 136)

    A.　True

    B.　False

51. In Wagner's works, there is clear delineation between the arias and recitatives. (p. 136)

    A.　True

    B.　False

52. The unifying thread within each act in Wagner's dramas is (p. 136)

    A.　A recurring rhythm

    B.　A return to the original tonic

    C.　An unending melody

    D.　A steady tempo

53. Why would Wagner want to remove the traditional places for applause? (p. 136)

_____

54. Wagner's opera cycle _Der Ring des Nibelungen_ consists of _____ operas. (p. 136)

55. Wagner's plots in the _Ring_ cycle portray (p. 136)

    A.   His devotion to his wife

    B.   His philosophical beliefs about society

    C.   His desire to make a lot of money

    D.   Wholesome, family entertainment

56. The most significant innovation in Wagner's operas is his special use of _____. (p. 137)

57. Wagner's melodic fragments that are used to represent characters, objects, or feelings are called _____. (p. 137)

58. The above named themes are treated symphonically, meaning that they are _____ or _____ as the drama unfolds. (p. 137)

59. Why are these themes altered throughout the entire cycle of operas? (p. 137)

_____

60. Wagner's harmonies are typically rich and chromatic and full of dissonance and tension. (p. 137)

    A.   True

    B.   False

61. Wagner's orchestra is used to provide descriptive colors within a small dynamic range. (p. 137)

    A.   True

    B.   False

62. Why are powerful voices necessary for Wagner's operas? (p. 137)

_____

63. What artistic movement followed in the wake of the Napoleonic Wars? (p. 141)

_____

64. This artistic movement was intended to reinforce _____ _____ in the arts. (p. 141)

65. Name two ways in which composers expressed themselves in this artistic movement. (p. 141)

    A.   _____

    B.   _____

66. This artistic movement partly arose as a reaction against the dominance of _____, _____, and _____ in European music. (p. 141)

67. The group of composers who made the greatest impact in nationalism were (pp. 141-142)

   A.   The Bohemian Three

   B.   The Finnish Four

   C.   The Russian Five

   D.   The Chicago Seven

68. Which of the following were members of the above named group? (p. 142)

   A.   Borodin and Balakirev

   B.   Dvorák and Smetna

   C.   Rimsky-Korsakov and Smetna

   D.   Sibelius and Grieg

69. Which of the following is characteristic of Mussorgsky's style? (p. 142)

   A.   Smooth, flowing melodies

   B.   Lightly dissonant harmonies

   C.   Traditional classical forms

   D.   Angular, dissonant harmonies

70. The work by Mussorgsky that is considered the most significant by this group is the opera

   _____ _____.   (p. 142)

CHAPTER 10, TWENTIETH-CENTURY MUSIC: 1900 to 1960

At the beginning of the 20th century there were several artistic movements that developed as composers pushed to the limits all the elements of music. Stemming from the extreme chromaticism of the late-19th century composers, such as Wagner, Liszt, and others, there was a revolution in harmony to the point that composers like Arnold Schoenberg began to write ATONAL music, i.e., music in which there is no tonal center or home key. Atonality led to a precisely organized type of composition called SERIALISM. The extended chords and harmonies that were introduced by Chopin, Liszt, and Wagner in the Romantic period were extended even further in the 20th century. The system of functional harmony was gradually broken down until composers such as Debussy were using chords more for the way they sounded than for any harmonic function. Debussy was one of the composers that was involved in the musical style known as IMPRESSIONISM.

There was also a revolution in the way in which composers viewed the whole time aspect of music. One of the leading composers who was seeking new avenues in musical time was Igor Stravinsky. Stravinsky's early music had very angular melodies and rhythms and his style for this music came to be known as PRIMITIVISM. This music has often been compared to the style of painting that Picasso was using at this same time. After World War II, Stravinsky and others reached back into the musical past to the forms and compositional techniques of the Baroque and Classical periods and, in some cases, back to the Renaissance and Medieval periods. By applying 20th century concepts of chord structure, chord progressions, orchestration, and melodic thought to Classical forms (such as sonata-allegro) and Baroque techniques (such as fugue), composers developed a style they called NEOCLASSICISM.

Another important development that occurred in music in the first half of the 20th century was the emergence of JAZZ styles from its folk and blues heritage into a unique genre. In the 1920s, Jazz began to exert an influence on art music as well. Composers such as George Gershwin, Aaron Copland, Igor Stravinsky, and others began to incorporate elements of the blues and jazz into their concert music. Jazz developed into three different styles in the first half of the 20th century: DIXIELAND, SWING, and BEBOP.

    I. New Images and Progressions (p. 146)

        A. Traditional chords and tonality were challenged at the beginning of the century

            1. Major and minor sonorities were stretched to include more dissonance

            2. Harmonies introduced by Chopin, Liszt, and Wagner were extended further

        B. Increased chromaticism and dissonance weakened the tonal center

            1. Eventually led to a breakdown in tonality

            2. Forward motion in music based on tonality also weakened

C. All stylistic developments in the early 20th century were searching for new sonorities and musical ideas that were not dependent on tonality

II. Impressionism (pp. 146-150)

    A. A musical style at the turn of the 20th century that emphasized tone color, sonority, and image

    B. The goal of impressionism was to express one's feelings or impressions of reality

    C. Impressionists had a new approach to chord structure and function

        1. Traditional chord constructions of stacked thirds were extended

        2. New chord constructions using fourths and fifths were introduced

        3. Chords were free of the traditional concepts of resolution

            a. The resolution of a dominant chord was less important than how it sounded

            b. The sound of two chords in relation to each other was more important than traditional chord resolution

        4. The relationship of consonance and dissonance changed

            a. A chord was considered dissonant in relation to the chords around it

            b. Consonance and dissonance became more relative to each other

    D. CLAUDE DEBUSSY (see biography, pp. 147-148)

        1. The leading composer of the impressionist style

        2. Strongly influenced by the French symbolist poets (e.g., Mallarmé, Verlaine)

        3. Typically, the orchestra is used for its coloristic possibilities

        4. Music is often shaped by the Debussy's personal perceptions of things

        5. Debussy's use of exotic scales further weakened the tonal center

            a. WHOLE TONE SCALE

                i. A scale that divides an octave into equal whole steps

                ii. Negates the natural perfect fourth and perfect fifth intervals

            b. Eastern scales such as the PENTATONIC SCALE

            c. These scales served to enhance Debussy's harmonic vocabulary

        6. Debussy's ability to create beautiful sonorities make his works favorites in this style

        7. LISTENING NOTES: *Prélude á l'après-midi d'un faune* (*Prelude to the Afternoon of a Faun*, pp. 148-150)

III. Nationalism Continues (p. 150)

    A. Nationalism played an important role in Stravinsky's first period style

        1. Uses folk songs and dances in his ballets (e.g., *Petrushka*)

        2. Uses folk tales as the basis of his ballets (e.g., *The Firebird*)

        3. Works capture the spirit of Russian life and culture

    B. Stravinsky was the most famous Russian nationalist composer after Mussorgsky

IV. Primitivism (pp. 150-154)

    A. 20th century musical style influenced by primitive works of art

    B. Music was an aggressive break from romanticism in music

    C. Music consisted of several disturbing or dissonant innovations

        1. Angular melodies

        2. Pounding, irregular rhythms

        3. Sharp dissonances

        4. Unique orchestral colors

    D. IGOR STRAVINSKY (see biography, pp. 153-154)

        1. The leading composer of the primitive style

        2. His ballet *The Rite of Spring* is an excellent example of the style

            a. Choreography was angular and almost grotesque

            b. Costumes were made of brown burlap

            c. The music was so startling that fighting erupted at the premiere of the work

        3. LISTENING NOTES: *Le Sacre du printemps* (*The Rite of Spring,* pp. 151-153)

V. Neoclassicism (pp. 154-157)

    A. Inspired by the restraint and control exhibited in the music of the 18th century

    B. Partly a response to the overly emotional music of the late 19th century

    C. Characteristics of neoclassical style

        1. 18th century characteristics

            a. Forms

                i. Sonata-allegro form

                ii. Minuet and trio

            b. Techniques

                i. Fugue

                ii. Canon

            c. Genres

                i. Dance suites

                ii. Concertos

                iii. ABSOLUTE MUSIC, music not associated with a story or program

        2. 20th century characteristics

            a. Harsh, dissonant harmonies

            b. Unique orchestrations and tone colors

            c. Rhythmic and melodic angularity

D. MUSICOLOGY developed in the 20th century

    1. Studies the stylistic development of music

    2. Developed from an interest in plotting the growth of new styles

    3. Also dependent on researching the development of older musical styles

    4. ETHNOMUSICOLOGY, the study of music specific to different cultures

E. BÉLA BARTÓK (see biography, p. 155)

    1. An important composer in the neoclassical style

    2. Also a renowned ethnomusicologist

        a. Studied the folk music of his native Hungary

        b. Blended elements from Hungarian folk music with modern composition

        c. Rarely quoted folk material, but used its structure and spirit in his works

    3. A unique and personal musical style

        a. Dissonance is often severe and almost atonal

        b. Music retains threads of tonality

        c. Wrote in traditional formal structures

        d. Melodies and rhythms were inspired by folk music

        e. Accompaniments used highly developed chordal and rhythmic structures

    4. LISTENING NOTES: *Concerto for Orchestra*, First movement: Introduction--Andante non troppo; Allegro vivace (pp. 156-157)

VI. Expressionism and Serialism (pp. 158-161)

A. EXPRESSIONISM

    1. Artistic style in which artists attempt to show their innermost thoughts and feelings

    2. Considered an extension of romanticism

    3. Expressions of feelings were often distorted, explosive

    4. Musical topics included frustration, anger, guilt, and terror

    5. Music became increasingly atonal

    6. ARNOLD SCHOENBERG (see biography, p.159)

        a. A Viennese composer, one of the leaders of expressionism

        b. Developed a new vocal technique called SPRECHSTIMME (speech voice)

            i. Voice half sings, half speaks the melody

            ii. Similar to animated speech

            iii. Enhances the images in expressionist music

        c. LISTENING NOTES: "Mondestrunken" ("Moonstruck") from *Pierrot Lunaire* (*Crazy Pierrot*, p. 160)

    7. ALBAN BERG (see biography, Topic 3, p. 238)

        a. Viennese composer, student and friend of Schoenberg

      b.   LISTENING NOTES: *Wozzeck,* Act III, Scenes 4 and 5 (Topic 3, pp. 239-241)

B.   In the hands of Arnold Schoenberg, atonality led to SERIALISM

    1.   A compositional style in which the twelve chromatic pitches are freed from the necessity of a tonal center

    2.   The twelve chromatic pitches are arranged in a melodic SERIES or TONE ROW

        a.   The row is the basis of a serial composition

        b.   The order of the notes in the row determine the order in which they appear in the composition

        c.   Chords are built from adjacent notes in the row

        d.   The series can be played:

            i.   Forward--Original Row

            ii.   Backwards--Retrograde

            iii.   Upside down--Inversion

            iv.   Upside down and backwards--Retrograde inversion

            v.   The row can start on another pitch--Transposition

        e.   No single pitch is supposed to sound more stable than another

    3.   Serialism is also known as TWELVE-TONE TECHNIQUE and DODECAPHONY

    4.   Later composers began to serialize more musical elements besides pitch

        a.   Rhythms

        b.   Dynamics

        c.   Timbres

C.   Developments in American music

    1.   New experimental techniques were being developed by composers Charles Ives and Henry Cowell

    2.   Experimented with TONE CLUSTERS on the piano

        a.   Several notes separated by the interval of a second

        b.   Played simultaneously to create a cluster of dissonance

        c.   Clusters may be played with the palm of the hand, the forearm, or a board

    3.   These composers were expressing the experimental mood that was developing in America in the early part of the century

VII. Blues and Jazz (1900-1950; pp. 161-171)

A.   Jazz developed from the combination of many musics brought to America

B.   Two important elements from West Africa helped in the development of jazz

    1.   Emphasis on complex POLYRHYTHMS

        a.   Two or more rhythms played simultaneously

        b.   Rhythms often conflict and blur the beat

2. Greater participation in the musical experience

    a. Listeners were expected to join in the music by singing, dancing, hand clapping

    b. Music was present in work, worship, and at rest

    c. A sophisticated relationship developed between the lead singer and the people who responded: CALL AND RESPONSE

3. These elements combined with European musical structures

C. Plantation owners could and did control the amount and type of music the slaves used

    1. Some were forbidden to perform their own music

    2. Some were allowed to use their own instruments but not their traditional melodies or rhythms

    3. European melodies were unknown to the slaves

    4. European harmonies were complex and confusing

D. The simplification of African rhythms and melodies and the simplification of European harmony led to a unique type of folk music: the BLUES

    1. A combination of the rhythmic freedom of call and response and the structure of chord progressions

    2. BLUE NOTES

        a. A pitch that is slightly lowered for expression

        b. Generally the third and seventh pitches of the major scale are lowered or "blued"

    3. Early blues performers used whatever instruments were on hand

        a. Washboards

        b. Spoons

        c. Harmonicas

        d. Guitars

E. Two categories of blues developed

    1. COUNTRY BLUES

        a. Sparse accompaniment, usually just a guitar

        b. Rhythmically and metrically free

        c. Singing style is equally free and expressive

        d. Texts typically dealt with the hardships of the downtrodden

        e. EXAMPLE: Robert Johnson, *Hellhound On My Trail*

    2. CITY BLUES

        a. More controlled than country blues

        b. Stricter use of meter

        c. Singing style is more refined

        d. Several musicians accompany the singer with horns and rhythm instruments

   e. EXAMPLE: Bessie Smith and Louis Armstrong, *St. Louis Blues*

F. Blues is still influential on today's music

  1. Several artists have established their own personal styles based on the blues

  2. Blues inflections are present in all styles of folk and commercial music

  3. Although the blues has developed new sounds, the basic simple structure has remained the same

G. Blues and Jazz Piano Styles

  1. The piano was very influential on the development of jazz

  2. BOOGIE WOOGIE

   a. A piano blues style popular in the 1930s

   b. Built on a left-hand OSTINATO (repeated melodic and rhythmic figure), usually consisting of eight notes

   c. The right hand played syncopated RIFFS (melodic motives)

   d. EXAMPLE: Meade "Lux" Lewis, *Honky Tonk Train*

  3. RAGTIME

   a. Developed from European dance forms

   b. Music is not improvised as is boogie woogie

   c. Strict form, usually AA BB CC DD

   d. Characterized by the left-hand pattern of a low note followed by a chord beneath a loose, syncopated style in the right hand

   e. EXAMPLE: Scott Joplin, *Maple Leaf Rag*

  4. STRIDE

   a. A more improvisatory style of piano music based on ragtime

   b. Popular in the late 1920s and the 1930s

   c. EXAMPLE: Art Tatum (see biography, p. 163), *Willow Weep for Me*

H. DIXIELAND

  1. An instrumental style of jazz that developed by the 1920s and remains popular

  2. Developed in New Orleans but spread north

  3. All instruments improvise melodies and rhythms to create a balanced texture: COLLECTIVE IMPROVISATION

  4. The most common instrumentation is for six players

   a. Trumpet (or cornet) is the most dominant instrument, plays the main melody

   b. Clarinet improvises a complementary melody above the trumpet

   c. Trombone plays a slower melody beneath the trumpet, helps define the harmony

   d. Drums provide rhythm and accent

   e. Piano provides rhythm and harmony to accompany the winds

   f. Tuba (later the string bass) supply the harmonic foundation and simple melodic ideas

  5. LISTENING NOTES: Louis Armstrong and his Hot Five, *West End Blues* (p. 165)

I. SWING

  1. A jazz style that developed in the late 1920s

  2. Began as experiments in instrumentation by composers such as Fletcher Henderson

  3. Led to a change in the basic ensemble: the Big Bands

   a. Band size grew from six to fifteen or more

   b. Organized in sections like an orchestra (sometimes called dance orchestras)

   c. Each section replaced one of the winds of the Dixieland combo

    i. Saxophone section, players also played clarinet

    ii. Trumpet section, four or five players

    iii. Trombone section, four or five players

    iv. Rhythm section--bass, drums, and piano

  4. Collective improvisation was impossible, written compositions were necessary

  5. Benny Goodman (see biography, pp. 166-167)

J. The Rhythm Section

  1. By the time swing became the dominant jazz style, the rhythm section became more clearly defined

  2. Rhythm section provided the basis for the swing style

   a. Two equal-valued notes played as long-short rather than even

   b. Melodic lines swing with this rhythm

   c. Some singers and instrumentalists played slightly behind the beat: LAYBACK

  3. Instruments of the rhythm section became standardized in the swing era

   a. Drums

    i. Maintains a steady pulse

    ii. Adds color through the use of cymbals, tom-toms, and bells

   b. Bass

    i. Helps provide the metric pulse

    ii. Supplies the fundamental harmonic progression

   c. Guitar and/or piano supply chords and rhythm in a style called COMPING

    i. Used to fill in the texture

    ii. Chords and rhythms *comp*lement the melodic instruments

    iii. Often an improvised accompaniment

  4. The swing period produced many great bands and soloists

   a. A great jazz performer had to be an expert improviser

   b. Band leaders required their soloists to add personality to the band

5. LISTENING NOTES: Duke Ellington (see biography, Topic 7, pp. 283-284),

   In a Mellotone (pp. 168-169)

6. LISTENING NOTES: Ellington, *Sophisticated Lady* (Topic 7, p. 285)

K. BEBOP

1. Jazz musicians in the 1940s revolted against the confinement of the swing style

2. Characterized by technical virtuosity and angular compositions

3. Virtuoso techniques combined with a thorough background in music theory

4. Based on songs from the swing era often with new melodies

5. Compositions were often A A B A song form

6. Emphasized fast and powerful improvisation

7. Other style characteristics of bebop include

   a. WALKING BASS

      i. Rhythmic/melodic bass line

      ii. One note is played on each beat of a measure

      iii. Notes move in a conjunct, scale pattern within the harmonic progression

      iv. Provides harmonic support for the rest of the ensemble

   b. BOMBS (DROPPING BOMBS)

      i. A drumming technique in bebop

      ii. Accented notes that do not correspond with other rhythmic ideas in the ensemble

      iii. Supply energy and excitement to the performance

8. LISTENING NOTES: Charlie Parker (see biography, pp. 169-170), *KoKo* (pp. 170-171)

EXERCISES

1. Listen to the third movement of *Three Nocturnes* by Claude Debussy; this movement is called "Sirènes" ("Sirens"). How does Debussy use the orchestra in this movement? What kinds of instrumental timbres are present in this movement? How is the women's chorus used? How does the chorus contribute to the overall texture and sound of this movement? Why did Debussy name this movement "Sirens"? Is there a noticeable form in this movement? If so, what is the form? Does Debussy follow established formal designs (such as ternary, binary, and so on)? What kinds of images does this movement evoke? What can be said about other musical elements, such as MELODY, TEXTURE, RHYTHM, METER, MODALITY, and HARMONY?

2. Listen to the opening movements of the following ballets by Stravinsky: *Petrushka*, *Pulcinella*, and *Agon*. Listen closely to the orchestrations and instrumentations of each ballet. Do you hear any similarities in regards to the way Stravinsky uses the orchestra? What are the differences between these ballets? Do the differences arise from compositional techniques or in the way in which Stravinsky uses the musical elements at his disposal? How does Stravinsky approach the following musical elements in each of these pieces: FORM, HARMONY, MELODY, RHYTHM? Which of these ballets seem to you to be the most effective for dancing? Why? How do these ballet excerpts compare or contrast with *The Rite of Spring* ?

3. Listen to the third movement of *Five Pieces for Orchestra, Op. 16* by Arnold Schoenberg. This movement is variously called "Farben" ("Colors"), "Morning by a Lake," and "The Changing Chord." Knowing that Schoenberg is an EXPRESSIONIST composer, why do you suppose he would attach such an impressionistic name as "Colors" or "Morning by a Lake" to this composition. To what do you think the name "Colors" is referring? What do you hear in the piece that suggests the name "The Changing Chord?" Is there a sense of tonality present in this work? Compare the sound of Schoenberg's orchestra in this piece to the sound of the orchestra in Wagner's *Götterdämmerung* excerpt. Are there similarities in the orchestral texture? Finally, can you detect a formal structure in Schoenberg's piece?

4. Listen to the tune *Parker's Mood* by Charlie Parker. What instruments are playing this tune? What is the vehicle of this piece? (A vehicle is a song type--strophic, through-composed, standard song form, 12-bar blues, etc.). How many times through the vehicle do Parker and his group play? What instruments play improvised solos? How many times through the vehicle are the solos? What kind of mood does the music evoke? How does this piece compare with the recording of *KoKo* ? What are the differences? What are the similarities? In both songs, how does the rhythm section support the other performers?

STUDY QUESTIONS

1. By the beginning of the 20th century the major and minor modes had been stretched by increased _____. (p. 146)

2. Increased use of chromatic harmonies and melodies resulted in a breakdown of (p. 146)

    A. Tonality

    B. Meter

    C. Timbre

    D. Rhythm

3. The musical style that emphasizes tone color and sonority is (p. 146)

   A.   Expressionism

   B.   Primitivism

   C.   Impressionism

   D.   Serialism

4. The principal composer of the above named style is _____. (p. 146)

5. What intervals, besides thirds, were used as harmonic building blocks? (p. 146)

   A.   _____

   B.   _____

6. Although the new chords may sound similar to the traditional chords, the new chords are free of

   traditional concepts of _____. (p. 146)

7. The most important quality of a chord in this style is (p. 147)

   A.   The number of pitches in it

   B.   The resolution of that chord

   C.   The number of times it is used in a composition

   D.   The way that chord sounds in relation to those around it

8. The French poetic style that exerted a great influence on this style of music was

   _____. (p. 147)

9. By what musical means did Debussy help weaken the idea of a tonal center? (p. 147)

   _____

10. The scale in which there are no half steps is (p. 147)

    A.   Chromatic scale

    B.   Dorian scale

    C.   Whole tone scale

    D.   Blues scale

11. Debussy's *Prélude á l'après-midi d'un faune* is based on a poem by _____. (p. 148)

12. Nationalism is present in Stravinsky's _____ style period. (p. 150)

13. A ballet by Stravinsky that illustrates the spirit and culture of Russian life is _____. (p. 150)

14. Stravinsky's most famous ballet, *The Rite of Spring*, is an example of (p. 150)

    A.   Expressionism

    B.   Primitivism

    C.   Impressionism

    D.   Serialism

15. The most notable musical characteristics of the above named style are (p. 150)

    A.   _____   C.   _____

    B.   _____

16. The audience openly accepted *The Rite of Spring* when it first premiered in Paris. (p. 150)

    A.   True

    B.   False

17. The style of *The Rite of Spring* was an aggressive break from Romanticism. (p. 150)

    A.   True

    B.   False

18. The characteristics of neoclassicism are equally based on _____ and
    _____. (p. 154)

19. Neoclassicism was in part a response to what? (p. 154)

    _____

20. Neoclassicism is a combination of 20th-century _____ and 18th-century
    _____. (p. 154)

21. The use of absolute musical forms indicate a desire for _____ and
    _____ found in 18th-century absolute music. (p. 154)

22. The study of historical and theoretical musical styles is called _____. (p. 156)

23. The study of music within an ethnic group or culture is called _____. (p. 156)

24. The composer who was a brilliant composer and ethnomusicologist was (p. 156)

    A.   Igor Stravinsky

    B.   Béla Bartók

    C.   Sergei Prokofiev

    D.   Paul Hindemith

25. Although his music may sound atonal at first, Bartók's music contains threads of tonality. (p. 156)

    A.   True

    B.   False

26. Bartók's melodies and rhythms are often inspired by the simplicity of _____ _____. (p. 156)

27. A German school of thought in which artists express their innermost thoughts is (p. 158)

    A.   Expressionism

    B.   Primitivism

    C.   Impressionism

    D.   Serialism

28. This movement was a reaction against romanticism. (p. 158)

    A.   True

    B.   False

29. A typical topic for this style art might be feelings of _____. (p. 158)

30. Music in this style is best expressed through _____. (p. 158)

31. A major composer who composed in this style was (p. 159)

    A.   Béla Bartók

    B.   Paul Hindemith

    C.   Igor Stravinsky

    D.   Arnold Schoenberg

32. A system of composition developed by the above named composer in which pitches are arranged and used in a specific order is called (p. 158)

    A.   Expressionism

    B.   Primitivism

    C.   Impressionism

    D.   Serialism

33. Two other names for this system of composition are (p. 158)

    A.   _____

    B.   _____

34. This system of composition effectively retains the feeling of tonality. (p. 158)

    A.   True

    B.   False

35. The basis of this system is the _____ of each note. (p. 158)

36. The order in which the pitches for a composition are arranged is called a _____ or a _____ _____. (p. 158)

37. In this system, chords can be built by (p. 158)

    A.   Stacking every other note of the series

    B.   Using adjacent notes in the series

    C.   Stacking every fourth note of the series

    D.   Chords are not used in this style of composition

38. The original series written backwards is called _____. (p. 158)

39. The original series played upside down is called _____. (p. 158)

40. Beginning the series on a different pitch is called _____. (p. 158)

41. A singing technique developed by Schoenberg for his compositions is called (p. 158)

    A.   Singspiel

    B.   Rezitativ

    C.   Sprechstimme

    D.   Arioso

42. In the above named style of singing, how does the vocalist present the text? (p. 158)

_____

43. Several notes that are separated by the interval of a second and played simultaneously is called a

    _____ _____. (p. 158)

44. Two American composers in whose works the above named technique appeared are

    _____ and _____. (pp. 158-159)

45. Two ways in which this technique can be performed on a piano are (pp. 158-159)

    A. _____

    B. _____

46. The two composers in question 44 above expressed the conservative mood of American art

    in the first half of the 20th century. (p. 159)

    A. True

    B. False

47. The beginning of jazz can easily be placed in time. (p. 161)

    A. True

    B. False

48. What two elements of West African music helped spark the development of jazz? (pp. 161-162)

    A. _____

    B. _____

49. The simultaneous use of two or more contrasting rhythms is called _____. (p. 161)

50. The relationship between a lead singer and his or her respondents is called _____.

    (p. 162)

51. The simplifications of what musical elements from Africa and Europe led to the development

    of the blues? (p. 162)

    Africa: _____

    Europe: _____

52. The blues combined the rhythmic freedom of _____ with the structure

    of _____. (p. 162)

53. "Blue notes" get their name from the lowering of pitch for expressive reasons. (p. 162)

    A. True

    B. False

54. Using a major scale as a basis, which scale degrees are typically "blued"? (p. 162)

    _____

55. The two categories of blues are _____ and _____. (p. 162)

56. Which of the following is NOT a characteristic of country blues? (p. 162)

    A.   Rhythmically free

    B.   Metrically strict

    C.   Sparse accompaniment

    D.   Free singing style

57. Which of the following is NOT characteristic of city blues? (p. 162)

    A.   Metrically free

    B.   Accompanied by a small group

    C.   Refined singing style

    D.   More control of musical elements

58. A blues piano style popular in the 1930s and using a repeated rhythmic figure is (p. 164)

    A.   Dixieland

    B.   Bebop

    C.   Boogie woogie

    D.   Stride

59. A highly improvisatory jazz piano style popular in the 1930s and related to ragtime is (p. 164)

    A.   Dixieland

    B.   Bebop

    C.   Boogie woogie

    D.   Stride

60. A repeated rhythmic figure that is usually played by the bass or piano left hand is called

    _____. (p. 164)

61. A jazz melodic motive from which larger melodic structures are built is called _____. (p. 164)

62. A jazz style that developed in New Orleans by the 1920s is (p. 164)

    A.   Dixieland

    B.   Bebop

    C.   Boogie woogie

    D.   Stride

63. The above named style is characterized by a balanced musical texture called _____

    _____. (p. 164)

64. The swing style of jazz was instigated by composers and arrangers who wanted to establish

    more control by the performer over the music. (p. 166)

    A.   True

    B.   False

65. The biggest change in the swing era was in the size of the ensemble. (p. 166)

    A.   True

    B.   False

66. The style of playing two notes of equal value with a long-short rhythm is called _____. (p. 167)

67. A melody that is played or sung slightly behind the beat is called _____. (p. 167)

68. The above named technique results in a feeling of improvisation. (p. 167)

    A.   True

    B.   False

69. What are the two main roles of the drummer in a rhythm section? (p. 168)

    A.   _____

    B.   _____

70. What are the main roles of the bass player in a rhythm section? (p. 168)

    A.   _____

    B.   _____

71. The rhythmic activity supplied by the piano and the guitar is called _____. (p. 168)

72. The jazz style that was a reaction against the confinement of swing is called (p. 169)

    A.   Dixieland

    B.   Bebop

    C.   Boogie woogie

    D.   Stride

73. The principal characteristics of the above named jazz style are (p. 169)

    A.   _____

    B.   _____

74. The two soloists who towered above all others in this style were _____

and _____. (p. 169)

75. A bass line in which a note is played on every beat of a measure and in a scale pattern is

called _____. (p. 171)

76. A drum technique in which heavily accented notes do not correspond with the other rhythmic

ideas is called _____. (p. 171)

CHAPTER 11, NEW MUSIC: 1960 to the Present

This chapter has addressed the experimental developments in academic music since 1960. Changes in music composition were based on philosophies about music and its role in society. Various methods of composition developed as composers expressed their views as to the place of music in society. Schools of composition discussed are: TOTAL SERIALISM, INDETERMINATE MUSIC, ELECTRONIC MUSIC, EXPERIMENTAL/THEORETICAL MUSIC, MINIMALISM, and NEOROMANTICISM. Developments in jazz in the 1950s and beyond were also discussed, including: THIRD STREAM, FUSION, and CROSSOVER.

I. Total Serialism (pp. 173-174)

    A. Expanded pitch serialization ideas of Schoenberg, Berg, and Webern

    B. Serial technique applied to other elements of music

        1. Rhythms

        2. Dynamics

        3. Timbre

        4. Articulations

    C. Composer's goal is to coordinate the various serialized elements through a comprehensive, often mathematical, plan

    D. Use of computers has made the possibilities of serial patterns nearly endless

    E. With computer, composer controls all variables of the music

    F. EXAMPLES

        1. Milton Babbitt, *Composition for Twelve Instruments*

        2. Karlheinz Stockhausen, *Gruppen*

II. Indeterminacy (pp. 174-177)

    A. Also called ALEATORY or CHANCE MUSIC

    B. Partially composed music

        1. Performer makes decisions concerning performance

        2. Decisions vary from what note to play to determine the overall structure

    C. Indeterminacy can be used with computer technology

        1. Programs written by composer may determine level of control toward the final composition

    D. Indeterminacy often used in combination with other compositional techniques, such as serial music

    E. JOHN CAGE (see biography, p 175)

        1. Important figure in indeterminate music

  2. Developed PREPARED PIANO

    a. Objects (e.g., screws, tools) placed in piano strings

    b. Percussive sound adds to texture of music

    c. Results in new and unpredictable sounds

  3. Studied philosophy of Zen Buddhism

    a. Moved away from traditional concepts of composition

    b. Led to writing compositions based on chance

    c. Began to include Oriental sounds (especially percussion) in his compositions

  4. Some examples of his music include elements that are beyond his or anyone's control: EXAMPLE: 4' 33"

  5. LISTENING NOTES: *Solo for Sliding Trombone* (p. 176)

III. Electronic Music (pp. 177-180)

 A. Developed through the merging of music and electronic technology

 B. TAPE MANIPULATION: sounds on magnetic tape used to create musical compositions

  1. Tapes can be spliced in different orders

  2. Tape speed can be altered faster or slower

  3. Tape can be played backwards

  4. Sounds on the tape can be distorted or filtered

 C. MUSIQUE CONCRÈTE

  1. Composed from recorded and electronically affected sounds subjected to tape manipulation

  2. Also may include electronically generated (SYNTHESIZED) sounds combined with recorded sounds

  3. EXAMPLE: Edgard Varèse, *Poème électronique*

 D. Composers combined electronically generated sounds with live performances: Babbitt, *Philomel*

 E. Early synthesized compositions could only be produced in large, expensive facilities (e.g., Columbia-Princeton Electronic Music Center)

 F. More complex computers and synthesizers are currently available to professional and amateur musicians

 G. Synthesizers have become important tools for composers in all musical styles

 H. LISTENING NOTES: Milton Babbitt, *Composition for Synthesizer* (p. 179)

IV. Experimental/Theoretical Music (pp. 180-182)

 A. Experimentation in music is a part of academic research

 B. Theory provides ideas on which a composition is based

C. Composers and performers look for new ways to free sound from traditional concepts

    1. New notational systems have been devised

    2. Extended performing techniques have been introduced

        a. Instrumentalists sing one part while playing another

        b. Instrumental ranges have been extended

        c. Virtuosity has been extended to extreme levels

        d. Some music written for player pianos because the level of complexity is beyond single players

D. Example: Robert Erickson, *General Speech*

V. Minimalism (pp. 182-183)

    A. Arose as an extreme reaction to the complexity of total serialism, electronic music, experimental music

    B. Partly reflects composers' interests in Eastern ideals and religions

    C. Can be described as simple levels of activity extended for large time periods

    D. LISTENING NOTES: Steve Reich, *Music for Mallet Instruments, Voices and Organ* (p. 182)

VI. Neoromanticism (p. 183)

    A. Research and experimentation led to detachment between composers and audiences

    B. Music based on theory and experimental performance

    C. Some composers have redirected the focus of their music to appeal to the average concert-goer

    D. Neoromantic music utilizes

        1. Emotional sensitivities similar to the Romantic period

        2. A return to tonality

    E. LISTENING NOTES: ELLEN TAAFE ZWILICH (see biography, Topic 5, p. 258), *Concerto Grosso 1985* (Topic 5, p. 259)

VII. Jazz: 1950 to the Present (pp. 184-190)

    A. Several different jazz styles developed in the 1950s

        1. Cool jazz (West Coast Jazz)

            a. Developed on the West Coast

            b. Softens aggressive edge of 1940s bebop

            c. Smaller melodic range in general

            d. More relaxed tempos

        2. Hard bop (Straight ahead jazz)

            a. Bebop style with less angular melodies

            b. Reintroduces elements of the blues to bebop

3. Third stream

    a. Combines elements of jazz and classical music

    b. Uses instruments associated with classical music (e.g., French horn, violin, flute)

    c. Uses compositional techniques associated with classical music (e.g., serialism, tone clusters)

    d. May use large ensembles like symphony orchestra

    e. Less patterned rhythm sections than other jazz styles

    f. Example: Miles Davis/Gil Evans, *Porgy and Bess*

4. Free jazz

    a. Developed in the 1960s

    b. Questions traditional concepts of melody, harmony and form

    c. Performers play anything at any point that they feel is musical

    d. Corresponds to experimental movements in classical music (avant garde)

    e. LISTENING NOTES: Ornette Coleman (p. 185), excerpt from *Free Jazz* (p. 186)

5. Fusion

    a. Combines elements of rock and jazz

    b. Rock elements:

        i. Rigid rhythm patterns

        ii. Hard-driving tempos and rhythms

        iii. Electronic instruments

        iv. Loud volumes

        v. Balance between soloists and rhythm sections

    c. Jazz elements

        i. Jazz formal structures

        ii. Jazz theory and harmonic progressions

        iii. Improvisation

    d. LISTENING NOTES: Michael Brecker (p. 188) and Don Grolnick, *Itsbynne Reel* (p. 189)

6. Crossover

    a. A jazz fusion style developed in the late 1970s

    b. Also incorporates commercial instruments

    c. Commercial style of jazz designed to reach a wide range of listeners

EXERCISES

1. Compose an aleatoric piece of music. Use any means to determine pitches, durations, rhythms, instrumentation, meter, melody, texture, and other musical elements. Perform it in class.

2. Listen to the composition *Different Trains* by Steve Reich. How does Reich use the human voice in this composition? How does the timbre of the voices compare with the timbre of the string quartet? Is there a discernible melody or theme in this composition? What musical element or elements are used to unify the composition, and how does Reich achieve this unity? Compare the different elements or ideas of the texts that are used for this composition. How does Reich relate the different text contents with each other? Does the music, either in the voices or in the quartet or both, relate in any way to trains? Explain your findings in a brief essay.

3. Listen to the free jazz composition *Enter Evening* by Cecil Taylor. Describe the instrumental sounds that you hear. Traditional instruments are used in this piece in dramatic, non-traditional ways. How would you describe the use of instruments in this piece? The piece is somewhat of a programmatic composition. What seems to be the program of this work? In what way do the instruments contribute to the program? Are all musical elements of this composition, such as MELODY, RHYTHM, METER, FORM, etc., free or can you detect some kind of organization in this work?

4. Listen to the song "La Fiesta" by Chick Corea on the recording *Return to Forever*. What elements of rock are present in this piece? What elements from jazz? Are there any other musical sources present in this example that contribute to the fusion of many styles? In what way do the various instruments and voices interact with one another and support one another? What instruments are used in this recording? How do they contribute to the overall texture of the composition? Do the rhythms and the meter suggest dance music to you? Is this piece strongly metric or rhythmic or not? How does the melody and harmonic progression contribute to your perception of this piece?

STUDY QUESTIONS

1. For post-1960 composers, the method of composition is as important as the sound of the music. (p. 173).
   A. True
   B. False

2. The serial works of Schoenberg, Berg and Webern were structured around _____. (p. 174)

3. The first composer to expand serial technique successfully to include rhythm, dynamics, and timbre was (p. 173)

   A.   Milton Babbitt

   B.   Steve Reich

   C.   John Cage

   D.   Edgard Varèse

4. An important serial composer who composed the work _Gruppen_ was

   _____ _____ (p. 174).

5. The computer is not well-suited to serial music. (p. 174)

   A.   True

   B.   False

6. Another term for indeterminate music is (p. 174)

   A.   Alliterative

   B.   Aleatory

   C.   Alimentary

   D.   Allomorphic

7. Unpredictable elements of indeterminate music ensure variety in performances. (p. 174)

   A.   True

   B.   False

8. Computers may be used in indeterminate music (p. 174)

   A.   To tell the composer that something is wrong

   B.   To tell the performer that something is wrong

   C.   To randomly select musical ideas from a bank of possibilities

   D.   Computers are not used in indeterminate music

9. The term for programming control away from the composer and into the computer is called

   _____ _____. (p. 174)

10. A leader in indeterminate music was (p. 174)

    A.   Michael Brecker

    B.   Ellen Zwilich

    C.   John Cage

    D.   Ornette Coleman

11. A piano in which small objects are placed between the strings is said to be

    _____. (p. 174, 177)

12. Cage's compositional style was influenced by his studies in Zen Buddhism. (p. 175)

    A.   True

    B.   False

13. The composition 4' 33" (p. 175, 177)

    A.   Was written on a piece of paper 4 feet, 33 inches long

    B.   Is determined by the environmental sounds of the audience

    C.   Involves the random playing of 4 radios for 33 minutes

    D.   Is named after the longitude/latitude where it was written

14. In the piece *Solo for Sliding Trombone* the trombonist (p. 176)

    A.   Manipulates the tone quality with mutes

    B.   Plays mostly expressive melodies

    C.   Recites a speech by Douglas MacArthur

    D.   Plays entirely on pedal tones

15. Indeterminacy combines well with other compositional styles. (p. 177)

    A.   True

    B.   False

16. Recording sounds from nature and altering these recordings by splicing and distorting the sound is called _____ _____. (p. 177)

17. Music made from combining electronically generated sound and recorded natural sound is called _____ _____. (p. 177)

18. The composer of *Poème électronique* is (p. 178)

    A.   Milton Babbitt

    B.   Karlheinz Stockhausen

    C.   Edgard Varèse

    D.   Pierre Boulez

19. Instruments that generate sound electronically are called _____. (p. 178)

20. An important electronic music facility in the 1960s was the Yale-Princeton Electronic Music Center. (p. 178)

    A.   True

    B.   False

21. Babbitt's *Composition for Synthesizer* (p. 179)

    A.   Combines synthesized sound with live performance

    B.   Is modeled after the work of Varèse

    C.   Uses serialized rhythms

    D.   Is expressively tonal

22. The most common product of experimentation is (p. 180)

    A.   New instruments

    B.   Failure

    C.   New performance techniques

    D.   Historical significance

23. Robert Erickson's *General Speech* integrates music, _____ and _____. (p. 181)

24. Experimentation in composition gave rise to extended performance techniques. (p. 181)

    A.   True

    B.   False

25. What is the object of composing pieces that are physically impossible to play? (p. 181)

    _____

    _____

26. Because no single person can play the complex meters and rhythms, some works are written

    for (p. 181)

    A.   Prepared piano

    B.   Two-handed piano performance

    C.   Player piano

    D.   Advanced virtuosos

27. Experimental composers and performers try to free sound from

    _____ _____. (pp. 181-182)

28. Minimalism is a reaction to the complexities of total serialism. (p. 182)

    A.   True

    B.   False

29. What is the purpose of having six vocalists sing one chord for almost sixty minutes in Stockhausen's

    Stimmung ? (p. 182)

    _____

    _____

30. Stockhausen's *Stimmung* is representative of minimalism. (p. 182)

    A.   True

    B.   False

31. Minimalism also reflects a new interest in _____ _____. (p. 182)

32. Composer Steve Reich's repetitive style has been influenced by his study of _____

    _____. (p. 182)

33. Reich's *Music for Mallet Instruments, Voices and Organ* has a strong sense of tonality. (p. 182)

    A.   True

    B.   False

34. Which of the following is a minimalist composer? (p. 182)

    A.   Arnold Schoenberg

    B.   Krzysztof Penderecki

    C.   Robert Erickson

    D.   Philip Glass

35. Experimental and theoretical music is generally easily understood by the average

    concert-goer. (p. 183)

    A.   True

    B.   False

36. Modern music that incorporates a sense of emotion similar to the Romantic period is called

    _____. (p. 183)

37. For her works, composer Ellen Zwilich has been awarded the (p. 183)

    A.   Pulitzer Prize

    B.   Nobel Prize

    C   Academy Award

    D.   Grammy Award

38. Music by composers like Zwilich and others has reopened communication between artist and

    audience. (p. 183)

39. The type of jazz that softened the aggressive elements of bebop is called (p. 184)

    A.   Third stream

    B.   Hard bop

    C.   Cool jazz

    D.   Free jazz

40. The type of jazz that added blues elements to bebop is (p. 184)

    A.   Third stream

    B.   Hard bop

    C.   Cool jazz

    D.   Free jazz

41. Third stream jazz united elements of jazz with elements of _____. (p. 184)

42. List two musical elements that might be present in third stream jazz. (p. 184)

    _____

43. The jazz style that questions traditional jazz styles is (p 184)

    A.   Third stream

    B.   Hard bop

    C.   Free jazz

    D.   Fusion

44. Free jazz incorporated a high level of _____. (p. 184)

45. Free jazz abandoned patterns of rhythms and meter of traditional jazz styles. (p. 184)

    A.   True

    B.   False

46. What is the difference between avant-garde classical music and free jazz? (p. 185)

    _____

    _____

47. The type of jazz that is combined with elements of rock is called (p. 188)

    A.   Third stream

    B.   Hard bop

    C.   Free jazz

    D.   Fusion

48. Which of the following might be an element of rock music used to create the type of jazz in question 47 above? (p. 188)

    A.   Unpredictable rhythm sections

    B.   Serialized pitch techniques

    C.   Massive levels of volume

    D.   Simple harmonic and formal structures

49. The wind controller that Michael Brecker plays on the song *Itsbynne Reel* is just an electric saxophone. (p. 189)

    A.   True

    B.   False

50. In more jazz-oriented jazz/rock groups, the rhythm section improvises around the soloist. (p. 190)

    A.   True

    B.   False

51. A jazz style which combines elements of rock and jazz with commercial instruments and recording techniques is called _____. (p. 190)

CHAPTER 12, ROCK: 1950 to the Present

This chapter deals with the development of rock music within the past forty years. Rock developed from several sources, most notably RHYTHM & BLUES, COUNTRY & WESTERN, THE BLUES, GOSPEL, and POPULAR MUSIC. It shares the same background as jazz, yet the two musical styles are very much independent of each other. Since 1950 there have been many hybrids of rock music, for instance JAZZ ROCK, COUNTRY ROCK, ART ROCK. There have also been increasing developments in recording techniques and recording technology and, perhaps more importantly, advances in the way in which the music has been disseminated to the public. Since the 1950s the recording business has gone from monaural, 10-inch, 78 r.p.m. records to stereo, 12-inch, 33 1/3 long-play albums to digital tape and compact discs. The venues in which the music appears have gone from the live AM radio broadcast and concert/dances to around the world satellite simulcasts and music videos on cable television. It has been an astonishing technical revolution. As the Grateful Dead so aptly put it: "What a long, strange trip it's been."

I. The Fifties (pp. 192-195)
   A. Popular music lyrics has been the most important element in popular music
      1. Music of Tin Pan Alley (1920s) provided the basis for popular song lyrics
      2. The lyrics in the popular ballads of the 1940s were very important to the audience
      3. In the 1950s lyrics were important in shaping rock's musical style
   B. Bill Haley and the Comets combined rhythm & blues with country to create a new vocal sound
   C. ELVIS PRESLEY (see biography, p. 194) intensified this sound by adding inflections from the black blues tradition
   D. RHYTHM & BLUES performers further defined the sound of 1950s rock 'n' roll
      1. Rhythmic blues dance form
      2. Led to the development of rock 'n' roll
      3. Amplified instruments
      4. Aggressive, vibrant style of music
   E. The tenor saxophone was the major melodic instrument
      1. Brass instruments rarely used
      2. Played a primary solo and accompaniment role
   F. Rhythm section followed the same format as the rhythm & blues rhythm section
   G. The twelve-bar blues structure and the rhythm & blues style are extremely important in the development of rock 'n' roll
      1. Provided rock with new vocal sounds, new lyrics, and new recording techniques
      2. The blues structure is so basic that songs are easily imitated and passed from one

113

person to another

      3. All recorded elements were imitated

         a. Music

         b. Vocal inflections

         c. Guitar styles

         d. Accompaniment figures

         e. No need for notated music, everything learned by ear

  H. The lines between jazz, rock, soft rock and rhythm & blues has always been indistinct

II. The Sixties (pp. 195-198)

  A. A new generation of listeners and several different cultural identities had an important influence on the direction of rock music

  B. THE BEATLES (see PAUL MCCARTNEY biography, p. 196)

      1. Their importance and lasting impact is unprecedented

      2. Explored the use of classical concepts

      3. Strongly experimental

         a. Recording techniques

         b. Jazz ideas

         c. Unusual sounds

      4. As the various members matured musically, their importance became more far-reaching

      5. Musical style falls into three periods

         a. Simple lyrics and musical arrangements

         b. Lyric symbols and electronic experimentation

         c. Rehearsed, studio-perfect performances dealing with mystical and abstract ideas

      6. After 1965, the group freely experimented with new sounds, new instrumental combinations, and new song structures

      7. An important breakthrough in rock music and recording technology was the album *Sgt. Pepper's Lonely Hearts Club Band* (1967)

         a. Concept album based on scenes from a concert with psychedelic overtones

         b. Contains a variety of instruments from sitars to a symphony orchestra

         c. Also makes use of crowd noises and sound effects for imagery

  C. Improvements in recording techniques encouraged more variety of rock styles

  D. Groups began to reflect diverse geographic locations and cultural background

      1. Surf music, e.g., The Beach Boys

         a. Flourished in southern California with the surfing culture

         b. Associated with good times and security

         c. Essentially reflects an untroubled world

2. Acid (psychedelic) rock, e.g., the Jefferson Airplane

   a. Flourished in northern California, notably San Francisco

   b. Associated with rebellion and demand for change

   c. Essentially reflects a dissident world

E. SOUL MUSIC

   1. Expresses another segment of cultural diversity

   2. Defined by a black musical tradition of slow rock

   3. A mixture of the emotions of black Gospel music with rhythm & blues

   4. A subcategory of soul music was MOTOWN

      a. Developed in Detroit (Motor Town = Motown)

      b. Style is named after a large record label in Detroit

      c. Essentially a black rock style that emphasizes rock rhythms

      d. Motown has contributed an impressive group of stars

         i. Stevie Wonder

         ii. Diana Ross

         iii. Smokey Robinson

         iv. MICHAEL JACKSON (see biography, p. 202)

F. The guitar has remained the most important instrument in rock music, further defined by Jimi Hendrix in the late 1960s

   1. Ability to manipulate electronic effects set a new standard for guitarists

      a. Use of wah-wah pedal for distortion

      b. Manipulation of pickup (toggle) switches and volume and tone controls

      c. Use of the tremolo bar

   2. Use of feedback as an improvisational tool both shocked and excited listeners

   3. Delivered an historic performance of *The Star Spangled Banner* at Woodstock using feedback almost exclusively

G. The effects of the Vietnam War was reflected in the music

H. Folk and folk rock singers of the 1960s and 1970s sang of individual freedom and respect

III. The Seventies (pp. 198-199)

A. Produced technological advances in music

   1. Better recording techniques

   2. More realistic product

   3. The imitation of live music in the studio was no longer the goal of record producers

B. The music business became a leader in experimenting with the storage, synthesis, and processing of sound

C. American and English musicians and promoters controlled the direction of rock music

D. English groups became models for American players to imitate

    1. The Rolling Stones

    2. The Who

    3. ELTON JOHN (see biography, p. 200)

E. Some musicians in America pursued a more folk-oriented style (e.g., Bob Dylan)

F. Jazz began to exert more influence on rock music

G. Progressive rock expanded musical structures and developed complicated textures

H. Rock approached fusion

    1. Groups started to use more brass instruments (e.g., Blood, Sweat, & Tears, Chicago)

    2. Blues and jazz ideas began to appear in standard rock 'n' roll structures

    3. Latin rhythms were introduced into rock (e.g., Santana)

IV. The Eighties (pp. 199-201)

A. Rock styles returned to a dance-oriented format: DISCO

    1. Dance style characterized by heavy bass drums on each beat

    2. Considered by some to be the popular music industry's response to progressive rock

B. Other styles developed in the early 1980s

    1. New Wave brought back an idea of simplicity

    2. Punk was an aggressive and loud style of basic rock

C. Virtuoso musicians began to bridge the gap between rock and jazz and vice versa

    1. John McLaughlin

    2. Herbie Hancock

    3. Jean-Luc Ponty

D. MULTITRACK recording procedures have redefined the group concept

    1. Individual parts are recorded separately and stored on tape

    2. Several tapes are mixed at a later date

        a. Blends instruments together into a musical whole

        b. Mixing is done electronically by recording engineers

        c. Most studios have 64 tracks available to record and mix later

    3. Recordings may use only two or three musicians but will sound like five or six

E. The job of producing is critically important and is often done by someone not in the band

    1. Producers' objectivity and knowledge about the industry is critical to success

    2. Important producers include

        a. George Martin for the Beatles

        b. Berry Gordy for the Motown label

        c. Quincy Jones for Michael Jackson

V. Heavy Metal and Rap (pp. 201-203)

   A. Heavy Metal

      1. Derived from acid rock of the 1960s

      2. Style characteristics

         a. High volume levels

         b. Thick electronic texture

         c. Vocals are typically mixed into the overall texture, not in the forefront

         d. Topics deal with rebellion, often focus on street culture

         e. Music is typically simple and direct

      3. The style has attracted a large following

   B. There is also an international underground of highly experimental rock

      1. Recordings are made locally and usually in tape format

      2. Primary areas of activity are on the American east and west coasts and in London

      3. Style characteristics

         a. Music is often caustic and angry

         b. There is a shift from mainstream cultural identity

         c. Subject matter is threatening and can be interpreted as revolutionary

         d. Seems to be most removed from academic environments

   C. Rap

      1. At the opposite end of the acceptance spectrum from metal

      2. Enjoys great popularity especially as an expression of black identity

      3. First appeared in the 1940s in association with bebop

      4. Style characteristics

         a. A rhythmic literary form rather than a developed musical structure

         b. Minimal harmonic motion

         c. Intensified rhythmic and metric patterns

         d. Speech patterns with minimal melodic shape are placed above the rhythm

      5. Strongly associated with cultural pockets in America

      6. Often seen as quasi-revolutionary and angry

VI. Music Video (pp. 203-204)

   A. The development of the music video was the most dramatic addition to rock in the 1980s

   B. Format is a theatrical musical entity

   C. Development of the video

      1. At first showed performances by groups

      2. Eventually became elaborate extensions of the song

   D. A video can often change one's perception of a song or the group who recorded it

E. Many groups only produce recordings and videos, but do not perform live

F. There has been quite a change from the early days of rock

    1. Music is now presented visually

    2. Visuals add new and extended interpretations of the music

G. Many rock styles are associated with various cultural developments

    1. Many styles show elements of folk culture

    2. Rock responds immediately to trends in society and culture

    3. Rock and jazz have produced styles that have become absorbed into the global commercial music industry

    4. New styles will continue to reflect societal changes, cultural shifts, and world conditions

EXERCISES

1. Read the chapter entitled "Five Styles of Rock 'n' Roll" in *The Sound of the City* by Charlie Gillett. What do you think of Mr. Gillett's statements? Do you agree with what he is saying or do you disagree with his statements? Does it make sense to you that Gillett categorizes the rock 'n' roll styles of the 1950s into five groups? Many other writers on rock music categorize the music from the 1950s as "Soft Rock or Pop" (such as Pat Boone, the doo wop groups, and so on), "Rockabilly" (Buddy Holly, Jerry Lee Lewis, and others), and "Mainstream Rock 'n' Roll" (everybody else, including Elvis Presley, Chuck Berry, Bill Haley and the Comets, Fats Domino, and the list goes on). (NOTE: These terms were taken from *Rock and Roll: Its History and Stylistic Development* by Joe Stuessy. There are several other rock books that use the same designations as Stuessy.) Can you make an argument that supports either of these categorizations?

2. Select at least two of the following songs from the lists below to listen to. Compare the original Rhythm & Blues or Blues versions to the Rock & Roll cover versions. What musical elements are similar in both versions? What are the differences in the versions? Describe these differences and similarities in words as best you can. Think of such elements as EMOTION or FEELING, PERFORMANCE STYLE, INSTRUMENTATION, and VOCAL ARTICULATION as well as musical elements such as RHYTHM, METER, TEXTURE, etc. (NOTE: Most, if not all, of these examples can be found on various volumes of the recordings *Blues Masters*, which are released by Rhino Records.)

SONG TITLE	ORIGINAL ARTIST	COVER ARTIST
That's All Right	Arthur "Big Boy" Crudup	Elvis Presley
Hound Dog	Willa Mae "Big Mama" Thornton	Elvis Presley

SONG TITLE	ORIGINAL ARTIST	COVER ARTIST
Shake, Rattle & Roll	Joe Turner	Bill Haley & the Comets
Tutti Frutti	Little Richard Penniman	Pat Boone
Crossroads	Robert Johnson	Cream
Bring It On Home	Sonny Boy Williamson	Led Zeppelin
You Need Love	Muddy Waters	Led Zeppelin (Whole Lotta Love)
Ball and Chain	Willa Mae "Big Mama" Thornton	Janis Joplin
Back Door Man	Howlin' Wolf	The Doors
Matchbox	Blind Lemon Jefferson	The Beatles
Love In Vain	Robert Johnson	The Rolling Stones

STUDY QUESTIONS

1. Jazz and rock are two closely related but distinctly different styles. (p. 192)

    A.   True

    B.   False

2. The decade in which jazz and rock combines was (p. 192)

    A.   The 1950s

    B.   The 1960s

    C.   The 1970s

    D.   The 1980s

3. List three musical styles that contributed to the development of rock. (p. 192)

    A.   _____

    B.   _____

    C.   _____

4. The music publishing area in New York that provided the basis for lyric writing in the 1920s was called _____ _____ _____. (p. 192)

5. The most important aspect of songs in the 1940s was the artist who sang them. (pp. 192-193)

    A.   True

    B.   False

6. The artists who sang the songs in the 1950s were most important in shaping the development of rock music. (p. 193)

    A.   True

    B.   False

7. What two musical styles did Bill Haley and the Comets merge to make a new vocal sound? (p. 193)

   A. _____

   B. _____

8. Elvis Presley imitated the vocal inflections of what musical style to help develop rock? (p. 193)

   _____

9. A rhythmic blues dance form that led to the development of rock 'n' roll is called _____

   _____. (p. 193)

10. What addition to the music gave early rock an aggressive sound? (p. 193)

    _____

11. The major melodic instrument in early rock 'n' roll was the _____ _____. (p. 193)

12. As in jazz, brass instruments were frequently heard in early rock 'n' roll. (p. 193)

    A. True

    B. False

13. The rhythm section of early rock 'n' roll bands was similar to that of the rhythm and blues bands.

    (p. 193)

    A. True

    B. False

14. The most basic formal structure of early rock 'n' roll is (p. 193)

    A. AABA song form

    B. 12-bar blues form

    C. Through-composed form

    D. Rondo form

15. In early rock 'n' roll, the music was learned mostly from notated parts. (p. 193)

    A. True

    B. False

16. The differences between soft rock and rock is clear and easy to define. (p. 194)

    A. True

    B. False

17. The differences between rhythm and blues and rock are indistinct. (pp. 194-195)

    A. True

    B. False

18. The group that best represented the rock style of the 1960s is _____. (p. 195)

19. Name two non-rock elements that the Beatles utilized in their music. (p. 195)

    A. _____

    B. _____

20. Which of the following is characteristic of the Beatles second period style? (p. 195)

    A. Mystical and abstract ideas

    B. Mostly instrumental songs

    C. Simple musical arrangements

    D. Beginning of studio experimentation

21. Which of the following is characteristic of the Beatles' third period style? (p. 195)

    A. Mystical and abstract ideas

    B. Mostly instrumental songs

    C. Simple musical arrangements

    D. Beginning of studio experimentation

22. The concept album that marks the height of experimentation in the studio was

    _____. (p. 197)

23. In the mid-1960s many rock groups began to reflect geographical locations and _____

    _____. (p. 197)

24. Surfing music was associated with _____ and _____. (p. 197)

25. Acid rock was associated with _____ and _____. (p. 197)

26. The music of the urban black community that mixed the emotions of gospel and rhythm and blues

    is called _____. (p. 197)

27. In what U.S. city was the above named music primarily produced? (p. 197)

    _____

28. The recording label that became the stylistic term for this music is _____. (p. 197)

29. The above named style strongly emphasized rock rhythms. (p. 197)

    A. True

    B. False

30. The most important instrument in rock music is _____. (p. 197)

31. The artist of the late 1960s who redefined the way in which the above named instrument

    was played was _____ _____. (p. 197)

32. This artist was especially known for his control and manipulation of _____. (p. 197)

33. The electronic distortion device that can sometimes sound like vocal inflections is (p. 197)

    A. Echo

    B. Wah-wah pedal

    C. Octave divider

    D. Phase shifter

34. The style of rock whose artists sang of individual freedom and respect was (p. 198)

    A.   Country rock

    B.   Jazz rock

    C.   Acid rock

    D.   Folk rock

35. The technological advances of the 1970s produced better recording techniques and consequently more _____ product. (p. 198)

36. The recording industry became the leader in experimenting with the _____, _____, and _____ of sound. (p. 198)

37. The rock style of the 1970s that expanded musical structures and textures was (p. 199)

    A.   Progressive rock

    B.   Funk rock

    C.   Heavy metal

    D.   New wave

38. What is the principal characteristic of disco? (p. 199)

    _____

39. An aggressive and loud style of basic rock in the 1980s was called _____ rock. (p. 199)

40. Jazz performers in the 1980s combined their virtuosic instrumental techniques with rock music to create _____. (p. 199)

41. The process of recording individual parts separately and mixing them at a later time is called (p. 201)

    A.   Fusion recording

    B.   Megatune recording

    C.   Multitrack recording

    D.   Microphone recording

42. One of the most critically important jobs in making a record is _____. (p. 201)

43. The rock style of the 1960s that led to heavy metal is (p. 201)

    A.   Country rock

    B.   Jazz rock

    C.   Acid rock

    D.   Folk rock

44. The two most prominent characteristics of heavy metal are (p. 201)

    A.   _____

    B.   _____

45. In the metal style, the vocals are mixed into the texture rather than being the focal point. (p. 201)

    A.   True

    B.   False

46. Lyrical topics in heavy metal are typically more _____ than those of mainstream rock. (p. 201)

47. An international underground music style combines elements of _____, _____, and metal. (p. 201)

48. The above named style is characteristically _____ and _____. (p. 201)

49 The musical style that is at the opposite end of the acceptance spectrum from metal is _____. (p. 203)

50. The above named style can be seen as an expression of _____ _____. (p. 203)

51. This style may be better described as (p. 203)

   A.   A lyrical poetic form

   B.   A rhythmic literary form

   C.   An arhythmic bebop form

   D.   An atonal poetic form

52. This style minimizes _____ motion and intensifies _____ patterns. (p. 203)

53. This style is characterized by speech patterns with minimal melodic shape. (p. 203)

   A.   True

   B.   False

54. The most dramatic development in rock in the 1980s was _____ _____. (p. 203)

55. This format can be seen as a theatrical music style. (p. 203)

   A.   True

   B.   False

56. Music videos are an important part of some performers' output because (p. 204)

   _____

57. Rock is typically slow to respond to trends in society and culture. (p. 204)

   A.   True

   B.   False

TOPIC 1:   IMPROVISATION AND COMPOSITION FROM THE KEYBOARD

I. Scarlatti, Liszt, and Evans (pp. 206-210)

   A.   In the last several hundred years keyboards have been the dominant instruments for composers

      1.   Provide opportunity to hear many parts simultaneously

      2.   Wider range of notes possible on keyboards than with most instruments

      3.   If writing for a large orchestra, the composer need not have the group present to compose

      4.   Composers can SCORE a work away from the group for which it is intended

   B.   A composer does not have to be an exceptional keyboard player, though many are

      1.   Many have the skill to develop musical ideas

      2.   Many ideas are discovered through the composer's performance

      3.   Composers create new ideas based on familiar hand patterns developed in practice

      4.   Melodies and themes are developed before being committed to paper

      5.   Composition is an intellectual and tactile experience

   C.   Many composers have been excellent performers with the ability to improvise spontaneously

   D.   IMPROVISATION

      1.   The instantaneous creation of music

      2.   Performers improvise many facets of the music

         a.   Melody

         b.   Harmony

         c.   Rhythm

         d.   Bass lines

         e.   Texture

      3.   Usually very expressive performances

      4.   Often contain unique stylistic elements based on the performer's technique

      5.   Melodic ORNAMENTS personalize each performance

         a.   Melodic devices used to accentuate a melodic idea

         b.   Used to decorate or enhance the melody

         c.   Ornaments may be rehearsed or freely added by a performer

         d.   Ornamentation occurs in every musical style period

         e.   Depending on the performer's ability, ornamentation may move a performance into the realm of improvisation

   E.   Composers often discover new melodic ideas while improvising

   F.   Improvisation is a means of releasing new musical ideas

   G.   Improvisation has been a constant source of excitement in music history

H.　Many composers were known for their skills as improvisers

　　1.　J. S. Bach, known in his lifetime as an improviser on organ

　　2.　Mozart, as a child performer often required to improvise new melodies for royalty

　　3.　Beethoven, first known in Vienna as an excellent improviser on piano

　　4.　Chopin, built a following in Paris with his improvisational skills

I.　Improvisation became increasingly scarce in classical music in the late 19th- and early 20th- centuries

　　1.　Composers did not often perform their own works; they wrote them for virtuoso performers

　　2.　Soloists did not feel that they could improvise a CADENZA in a concerto that was equal to the music written by the composer

　　3.　Soloists were often not composers themselves

　　4.　Performers may have not considered themselves worthy of improvising works by Beethoven or other major composers of the preceding periods

　　5.　Sections that had originally been improvised are now commonly rehearsed

J.　Improvisation has remained active with classical organists

　　1.　Church organists still improvise in sections of church services

　　2.　Accomplished improvisers develop material from the hymns used in the service

K.　GIUSEPPE DOMENICO SCARLATTI (see biography, p. 210)

　　1.　Known for his improvisational abilities on the harpsichord

　　2.　His compositions exhibit a flamboyant keyboard style based on improvisational techniques

　　3.　Many of his harpsichord sonatas (*ESSERCIZI*--Exercises) have dramatic swings in mood that are more like improvisation than a structured composition

　　4.　LISTENING NOTES: *Sonata in C-sharp minor*, K. 247 (p. 209)

II.　From Improvisation to Notation (pp. 210-214)

A.　The spirit of improvising on the piano translates to other instruments and ensembles

B.　FRANZ LISZT (see biography, p. 211)

　　1.　Known as one of the powerful pianists and improvisers of the late 19th century

　　2.　Equally known for his orchestral writings, especially his TONE POEMS

　　3.　Tone poem *Les Préludes*

　　　　a.　An example of Liszt's innovative orchestral writing

　　　　b.　Very emotionally charged work with interesting harmonic moments

　　　　c.　Some ideas were possibly developed from his piano technique

　　　　d.　Themes are varied using a technique called THEMATIC TRANSFORMATION

　　　　　　i.　Themes take on a different character each time they appear

　　　　　　ii.　These are reminiscent of thematic development used in long improvisations

　　　　e.　LISTENING NOTES: *Les Préludes* (pp. 212-213)

125

C. The degree of influence that improvisational techniques have on composers cannot be known

    1. Composers must have gained some insight and inspiration from their improvised ideas

    2. The musical ear of an improviser combined with the technical skill of a performer and composer have yielded much exciting music

III. Improvisation Continues (pp. 214-217)

    A. Improvisation did not vanish because it became less active in the concert hall

        1. Improvisation is a natural development for any musician

        2. Songs that are sung over and over are eventually changed

        3. These variations are essentially improvisations

    B. The most active musical styles for improvisation today are jazz and experimental classical

    C. Jazz has many STANDARDS that have become the basis for improvisation

        1. Based on songs from musicals or commercial music

        2. Considered standards because most jazz performers know the songs and they are standard to jazz literature

        3. Original melodies are replaced by new, improvised melodies

    D. There have been many great jazz pianists who each have a personalized style based on

        1. Ornamentation

        2. Inflection

        3. Use of music theory

    E. BILL EVANS (see biography, p. 217)

        1. Influential in developing a new improvisational style beginning in the 1950s

        2. Became a new model for his harmonic ideas and melodic sense

        3. Melodies were usually written in a commercial shorthand style; written melodies were accompanied by chord symbols with HARMONIC EXTENSIONS

            a. Notes that are dissonant to the three fundamental chord tones

            b. Theoretically related to the chord

        4. His compositional activities were centered around his improvisations

        5. Much of his improvisations have been preserved on recordings

        6. LISTENING NOTES: *Pavane*, based on a theme by Gabriel Faure, arranged by Claus Ogerman, improvisations by Bill Evans (pp. 215-216)

    F. A central point of improvisation is to introduce some form of unity or structure

        1. Determined by a song's chord structure

        2. Determined by a specific length of time

        3. Determined by a simple rhythm

    G. The freedom of improvisation varies considerably

        1. Ornamentation of a written melody

2. Interpretation is used freely and spontaneously in a performance

  a. Performance liberties exist in tempos and dynamics in notated music

  b. Free interpretation provides a powerful communication between performer and audience

  c. Listeners are generally receptive to music that sounds spontaneous and freely expressive

EXERCISES

1. Listen to a recording of the *Tocatta and Fugue in D minor* for organ by Johann Sebastian Bach. Does this music seem to have a sense of improvisation about it? Describe the melody of the tocatta. Is the melody shifted between the various ranges of the organ? Or is there a basic upper range melody that is supported by the lower parts? What type of texture is this? Do you hear recurring motives or themes throughout the tocatta? Does ornamentation seem to occur frequently to decorate the melody? In the fugue section, are there any motives or themes that remind you of the melody of the tocatta? How are the organ stops used to vary the sound of this work?

2. Listen to the *Transcendental Etude No. 4: Mazeppa* by Franz Liszt. Does this piano work seem to have improvisational qualities? Does this sense of improvisation, if any, occur in the melody? Harmony? Rhythm? Form? What is the texture of this piece like? How does this affect the perception of the piece?

3. Listen to at least three of the following pieces featuring jazz pianists. Compare the performances in regard to the performer's approach to improvising the melody. (In some examples, other jazz performers also improvise on the melody. Compare their work to that of the pianist who is featured.) Describe some of the techniques you hear as best as you can. How is rhythm or the beat treated by these performers? Do they remain close to the original melody or do the performers get far away from the original melody? Does the harmonic structure remain the same or is there some liberty to the chord progression? Compare other musical ideas such as the accompaniment in the left hand while the right hand improvises a melody.

  Earl Hines, *57 Varieties*

  Errol Garner, *Willow Weep for Me*

  Bud Powell, *A Night in Tunisia*

  Thelonius Monk, *Round Midnight*

  Chick Corea, *La Fiesta*

  Herbie Hancock, *Chameleon*

STUDY QUESTIONS

1. In the last several hundred years the dominant instruments from which composers prefer to work have been (p. 206)

    A.   Woodwind instruments

    B.   Keyboard instruments

    C.   String instruments

    D.   Brass instruments

2. The above instruments have been preferred because (p. 206)

    A.   Composers do not have to be able to play them well

    B.   They have a wide range of pitches

    C.   Every composer owns one

    D.   It is possible to hear more than one part at a time

3. The process of placing instruments into the musical texture is called _____. (p. 206)

4. A composer often discovers new musical ideas while performing. (p. 207)

    A.   True

    B.   False

5. _____ and _____ are often discovered and developed before ideas are put on paper. (p. 207)

6. Composition is both an intellectual and _____ experience. (p. 207)

    A.   Tactile

    B.   Religious

    C.   Rewarding

    D.   Foolhardy

7. The ability to create music instantaneously is called _____. (p. 207)

8. Many composers in the past have not been very good improvisers. (p. 207)

    A.   True

    B.   False

9. Improvisations usually have unique style elements because (p. 207)

    A.   They are played in the historical period style of the moment

    B.   They contain ideas specific to the performer's technique

    C.   They are free-form ideas based on scales and chords

    D.   They are not written down on paper

10. Texture can be improvised by all the musicians working together. (p. 207)

    A.   True

    B.   False

11. The musical elements that help personalize an improvisation are (p. 207)

    A.   Individual rhythms

    B.   Repeated motives

    C.   Melodic ornaments

    D.   Unique tone colors

12. The Baroque musical genre in which the singer would heavily ornament the return of the A section was called (p. 207)

    A.   Opera recitative

    B.   Da capo aria

    C.   Monody

    D.   Lieder

13. Complex motives and melodies are often discovered while improvising. (p. 207)

    A.   True

    B.   False

14. Composers such as Mozart and Chopin were often required to improvise on melodic ideas given to them (p. 208)

    A.   From a book of themes and melodies

    B.   From a published symphony or opera

    C.   Based on a well-known folk tune

    D.   By a member of the audience

15. These performances often were displays of _____ and technical skills. (p. 208)

16. An unaccompanied solo that is commonly associated with the concerto is called (p. 208)

    A.   A cadenza

    B.   A consequence

    C.   A consonance

    D.   A cappella

17. The above named solo is typically free in pulse and meter. (p. 208)

    A.   True

    B.   False

18. Which of the following did NOT contribute to the decline of improvisation in the 19th century? (p. 208)

    A.   Composers were not performing their own works

    B.   Soloists found it difficult to improvise a solo at a level equal to the composition

    C.   Audiences wanted to hear only that music which had been written down

    D.   Soloists were often not composers themselves

19. During the Baroque, Classical, and Romantic periods improvisation was the least exciting part of a performance. (p. 208)

   A. True

   B. False

20. Most classically trained pianists today are eager to improvise on stage. (p. 208)

   A. True

   B. False

21. The classical keyboard performers who have remained active improvisers in modern times are (p. 208)

   A. Concert pianists

   B. Church organists

   C. Vocal accompanists

   D. Instrumental accompanists

22. A common place to improvise in a church performance is (p. 208)

   A. During the sermon

   B. Before everyone has left for the day

   C. In between verses of a hymn

   D. During the processional

23. Creative church improvisers develop material that has been presented in _____. (p. 208)

24. The Baroque composer who was known during his lifetime as an improviser on organ was (p. 208)

   A. J. S. Bach

   B. F. Chopin

   C. D. Scarlatti

   D. W. Mozart

25. The Baroque composer known for his acrobatic skills on the harpsichord was (p. 208)

   A. J. S. Bach

   B. F. Chopin

   C. D. Scarlatti

   D. W. Mozart

26. Domenico Scarlatti referred to his keyboard sonatas as _____. (p. 209)

27. One of the most powerful pianists and improvisers of the late 19th century was (p. 210)

   A. Ludwig van Beethoven

   B. Frederic Chopin

   C. Richard Wagner

   D. Franz Liszt

28. The innovative orchestral composition *Les Préludes* is known as a _____ _____. (p. 210)

29. The process of changing a theme so that it takes on a different character each time it returns in a movement or work is called (p. 212)

    A.   Cyclic themes

    B.   Thematic transformation

    C.   Leitmotiv

    D.   Improvisation

30. The degree of improvisation that is inspired by a composer's technique is easy to figure. (p. 214)

    A.   True

    B.   False

31. Improvisation is a natural development for anyone who sings or plays music (p. 214)

    A.   True

    B.   False

32. The two musical styles most active in improvisation today are (p. 214)

    A.   _____

    B.   _____

33. At what point does indeterminate music require improvisation? (p. 214)

    _____

34. Favorite jazz songs that are the bases for jazz improvisation are called _____. (p. 215)

35. The jazz pianist who was influential in setting a new improvising style in the 1950s was (p. 215)

    A.   Duke Ellington

    B.   Scott Joplin

    C.   Bill Evans

    D.   Claus Ogerman

36. The compositional activities of the above named pianist were centered around (p. 215)

    A.   His improvisations

    B.   Newark, New Jersey

    C.   His experiences in the army

    D.   The jazz clubs of Kansas City

37. Notes that are dissonant to the fundamental three notes of a chord but still theoretically related to that chord are called _____ _____. (p. 215)

38. An important aspect of all levels of improvisation is some form of (p. 216)

    A.   Melodic shape

    B.   Unity

    C.   Tonal center

    D.   Rhythmic impetus

39. A limited form of improvisation is _____ of a written melody. (p. 216)

40. Freedom in _____ communicates a performance intensely to the listener. (p. 216)

41. Listeners are usually less receptive to music that sounds spontaneous or freely expressive. (p. 216)

    A.   True

    B.   False

TOPIC 2, COMPOSING FOR THE LARGE ORCHESTRA

I. Beethoven and Mahler (pp. 218-219)

    A. The modern orchestra has many colors and sounds available to it

        1. Ranges from solo instruments to subtle instrumental combinations

        2. Capable of large, loud sounds and small, delicate sounds

        3. The sound of the orchestra has changed with the addition of new instruments

    B. Beethoven (see Chapter 8)

        1. Introduced trombone, piccolo, and contrabassoon to the orchestra

        2. Combined orchestra and choir in the *Ninth Symphony*

    C. GUSTAV MAHLER (see biography, p. 225)

        1. Also used chorus and solo voices with orchestra

        2. Included new instrumental combinations

        3. Expanded the percussion section

        4. Introduced several new instruments to the orchestra

            a. Mandolin

            b. Guitar

            c. Celesta

            d. Cowbell

    D. Both Beethoven and Mahler were searching for new instrumental sounds

        1. New timbres from new instruments in the orchestra

        2. New combinations of traditional instruments

    E. Technical improvements of instruments influenced the direction of the orchestra

        1. Greater tone projection in the string instruments

        2. Introduction of valves on brass instruments

    F. Both Beethoven and Mahler are considered important in the development of the symphony

II. The Developmental Process (pp. 219-227)

    A. The symphonies of Beethoven and Mahler illustrate how composers can expand the basic structure of the symphony without weakening it

        1. Traditional structure of four movements was changed

        2. Relationship of each movement to the whole was developed

        3. The process of development was applied to structure as well as to themes and motives

    B. Beethoven, *Symphony No. 5 in C minor, Op. 67*

        1. Entire symphony can be reduced to a single, four-note MOTIVE

            a. A small musical unit

            b. A short, identifiable rhythm made up of a few pitches

2. The Fifth Symphony motive was described by Beethoven as "fate knocking at the door"

3. This symphony exemplifies organic composition

    a. A single idea is used throughout the large work

    b. The rhythm of the four opening notes occurs in all four movements

4. Other changes made by Beethoven in the Fifth Symphony

    a. Third movement is changed from a minuet to a scherzo

    b. The tension of the third movement is released only by the fourth movement

    c. The pause between the third and fourth movements is removed

    d. Themes from the third movement are recalled in the fourth movement

5. LISTENING NOTES: *Symphony No. 5 in C minor, Op. 67* (pp. 220-222)

C. Mahler's musical career

1. Besides symphonies also composed other large works

    a. Completed three operas

    b. Wrote several songs (Lieder) for voice and piano or orchestra

2. Most famous during his lifetime as an orchestra conductor

    a. Conducted large operatic works in Austria and Germany

    b. Mostly conducted the works of other composers

    c. Well-known for his interpretation of the operas of Mozart and Wagner

    d. Became director of the New York Philharmonic Society in 1908

    e. Also became the director of the Metropolitan Opera House in New York

3. His conducting success stemmed from Mahler's ability to understand and interpret historical and contemporary works

4. This gave him the background to manipulate instrumentation and structure in his own works

D. Mahler, *Symphony No. 6*

1. Extends the innovations of Beethoven

2. Uses organic themes and motives

3. The last movement is the culmination of the first three movements (like Beethoven)

4. A dominant element is the use of counterpoint, especially in the last movement

5. Grand themes in the first and last movements are contrasted with small ensemble sounds associated most often with CHAMBER MUSIC

6. The most dramatic quality of Mahler's music is his ability to control the huge orchestra

7. Like Beethoven, Mahler expanded the length and scope of the symphony

8. LISTENING NOTES: *Symphony No. 6* (pp. 225-227)

EXERCISES

1. Listen to *Symphony No. 1 in C minor* by Johannes Brahms and compare this symphony to the works studied in this topic chapter. How does Brahms's orchestra compare in size and instrumentation to that of Beethoven? To that of Mahler? Is Brahms's approach to orchestration (how he uses the instruments) similar or different to Beethoven or Mahler? Does Brahms develop themes and motives in the manner of Beethoven? What about the instrumental ranges? Compare the three composers' sense of tone color in their orchestras.

2. Listen to *Symphony No. 9 in E minor* by Antonin Dvorák. Compare this symphony to the Brahms symphony named above and to the Beethoven and Mahler symphonies discussed in this chapter. Does Dvorák have a similar approach as these other composers in regards to the symphony? What seems similar? What is different? Is there a recurring theme in this work that occurs in more than one movement? How does Dvorák's treatment of the orchestra compare with that of Beethoven? Brahms? Mahler? Does Dvorák's music seem to you to be progressive or conservative compared to the other composers discussed here? Why do you think this is so?

STUDY QUESTIONS

1. The tone colors of the modern orchestra range from _____ _____ to subtle _____ of instruments. (p. 218)

2. The sound of the orchestra has changed with the introduction of (p. 218)

    A.   A new conductor

    B.   Newly accepted instruments

    C.   Acceptable dissonances

    D.   Acceptable consonances

3. The instrument that has most recently found acceptance in the modern orchestra is (p. 218)

    A.   The glockenspiel

    B.   The sousaphone

    C.   The saxophone

    D.   The Wagner tuba

4. Three instruments that Beethoven introduced into the symphony orchestra were the _____, the _____, and the _____. (p. 218)

5. Beethoven also combined the _____ and the orchestra in his Ninth Symphony. (p. 218)

6. Mahler did not add choruses to his instrumental music. (p. 218)

    A.   True

    B.   False

7. Mahler expanded the (p. 218)

    A.   Percussion section

    B.   Brass section

    C.   Woodwind section

    D.   String section

8. Mahler also used mandolin and guitar in some of his symphonies. (p. 218)

    A.   True

    B.   False

9. In what ways did Beethoven and Mahler achieve new tone colors? (p. 219)

    A.   _____

    B.   _____

10. The string instruments of the 20th-century orchestra project a stronger tone. (p. 219)

    A.   True

    B.   False

11. Brass instruments were improved by the introduction of _____. (p. 219)

12. The symphonies of Beethoven and Mahler are good examples of how expanding the basic structure of the symphony weakens it. (p. 219)

    A.   True

    B.   False

13. What element of the traditional symphony became the first target for change? (p.219)

    _____

14. Beethoven and Mahler were also concerned with the relationship of each _____ to the whole. (p. 219)

15. With these composers, development is restricted to themes and motives. (p. 219)

    A.   True

    B.   False

16. The single element that Beethoven's Fifth Symphony can be reduced to is (p. 219)

    A.   The key of C minor

    B.   The tempo Allegro

    C.   The opening four-note motive

    D.   The duple meter of the first movement

17. A small musical unit consisting of a short identifiable rhythm and a few pitches is called (p. 219)

    A. An ostinato

    B. A motive

    C. A riff

    D. A cadence

18. Beethoven referred to the four-note motive of the Fifth Symphony as (p. 219)

    A. The Furies hounding his soul

    B. The bitterness of his deafness

    C. His anger at his nephew

    D. Fate knocking at the door

19. Beethoven's symphonic writing style exemplifies _____ composition. (p. 219)

20. In Beethoven's symphonies, the minuet is often replaced with _____. (p. 220)

21. The tension of the third movement of the Fifth Symphony is resolved by (p. 220)

    A. The final cadence of that movement

    B. The fanfare-like opening of the fourth movement

    C. Changing the mode of the trio from minor to major

    D. Gradually slowing the tempo of the third movement

22. This resolution is helped by removing the break between the third and fourth movements. (p. 220)

    A. True

    B. False

23. Besides using the opening motive in all four movements, the Fifth Symphony is further unified by (p. 220)

    A. Recalling themes from the third movement in the fourth movement

    B. Using the same tonal center in all four movements

    C. Using the same melody for transition sections of each movement

    D. Using sonata-allegro form in all four movements

24. A significant characteristic of Beethoven's style is deviation from standard forms. (p. 220)

    A. True

    B. False

25. Besides symphonies, Mahler wrote many songs that are accompanied either by piano or by _____. (p. 222)

26. During his lifetime, Mahler was most famous for (p. 222)

    A. His compositional skills

    B. His improvisational skills on the piano

    C. His conducting skills

    D. His music criticism

137

27. Mahler conducted mostly his own works. (p. 222)

    A.   True

    B.   False

28. Mahler was very well known for his interpretation of the operas of (p. 222)

    A.   Mozart and Beethovon

    B.   Mozart and Wagner

    C.   Brahms and Wagner

    D.   Schumann and Brahms

29. The two American musical groups that Mahler directed were (p. 222)

    A.   _____

    B.   _____

30. Mahler's understanding of historical and contemporary music gave him the background to
    manipulate _____ and _____ in his own works. (p. 222)

31. Mahler's own compositions had a great impact on musical society during his lifetime. (pp. 222-223)

    A.   True

    B.   False

32. An active musical ear is the activity of creative imagination. (p. 223)

    A.   True

    B.   False

33. The dominant element of Mahler's Sixth Symphony is _____ _____. (p. 223)

34. The above named technique gives new personality to the thematic material. (p. 223)

    A.   True

    B.   False

35. The grand themes of the first and fourth movements of the Sixth Symphony are contrasted with
    smaller ensemble sounds associated with _____ _____. (p. 223)

36. Mahler's Eighth Symphony calls for a huge orchestra, vocal soloists, and (p. 224)

    A.   A mixed chorus and a women's chorus

    B.   Two men's choruses

    C.   Two mixed choruses and a women's chorus

    D.   Two mixed choruses and a boy's chorus

37. The most dramatic quality of Mahler's music is (p. 224)

    _____

38. Both Beethoven and Mahler _____ the length and scope of the symphony. (p. 224)

TOPIC 3, WORDS AND MUSIC

I. Introduction (pp. 228-229)

    A. There have always been arguments concerning the roles of words and music

        1. Should music be subservient to the text

        2. Should words and music establish an equal partnership

        3. This issue resurfaces whenever there is significant musical change

    B. Words and early chant

        1. Texts were originally set in a one note per syllable style

        2. The music was monophonic, so the words were not impeded by musical activity

        3. MELISMAS (several notes per syllable) gradually became more important

            a. Emphasized specific words

            b. Ornamented special words or ideas

    C. Words and early polyphony

        1. A CANTUS FIRMUS was borrowed from a sacred text or chant to be the unifying element of a composition

            a. Chant melody slowed to a drone

            b. Text remained in Latin

            c. The words were mostly unintelligible because the syllables were so spread out

        2. Faster and more easily understood texts were sung above the slow cantus

        3. The thick, busy texture resulted in more focus on the music than on the words

II. Clement Jannequin and Word Painting (pp. 229-231)

    A. The interest of composers to describe words through sound is especially evident in Renaissance MADRIGALS

        1. Secular love poem popular in the Renaissance

        2. Set in a polyphonic texture with contrasting homophonic sections

        3. Frequently uses WORD PAINTING

            a. A word stressed musically to make it stand out from those around it

            b. Emphasis is to interpret the special meaning of the word

    B. Jannequin's chansons are clear examples of word painting

        1. LISTENING NOTES: Jannequin, *Chant des oiseaux* (*Song of the Birds*; pp. 229-230)

        2. The vocal text imitates the sounds of birds

    C. In the later Renaissance vocal music, especially sacred vocal music, intended to make the words stand out more clearly

        1. A more conservative approach to texture so as not to hide the words

        2. Less of the theatrical effects of word painting in madrigals and motets

D. Vocal music in the Baroque

   1. More focus on a single melodic line and continuo accompaniment

   2. New balance between words and music, MONODY

   3. Results in a more homophonic texture

   4. Frees words from the thick polyphonic texture of madrigals

   5. This did not eliminate vocal polyphony, as evidenced in the choral works of Handel and Bach

E. Vocal music in the Romantic period

   1. The Romantic period has some of the clearest examples of aligning music and words in the lieder of Schubert and others

   2. Lieder accompaniment and melodies interpreted the general meaning of the words

   3. Word painting was used to emphasize specific words

F. SPRECHSTIMME in the 20th century represents a return to the importance of the text

G. Popular music styles have different approaches to the text

   1. Country & western has always placed great importance on the words over the music

   2. Heavy metal places the vocal part within a thick texture where the words are hard to hear

   3. Rap is completely word oriented music

   4. Romantic ballads are based on the meaning of the words

   5. Dance music emphasizes the music first and the words second

   6. Most listeners focus on the words first and the music second

III. The Composer and the Libretto (pp. 231-232)

   A. Composers must consider many elements in choosing a song text

      1. Subject matter is the most important concern

      2. The text must also have musical potential

   B. The librettist is required to arrange the words into patterns

      1. Rhythms and sounds to stimulate the composer

      2. The actual sound of a word affects the tone and texture of a composition

         a. Some sound soft: "free," "man"

         b. Some are percussive or rhythmic: "people," "startle"

         c. Replacing words with synonyms changes the sound of the music

         d. Many argue that translating a text from its original language destroys the art of the original composition

   C. Repetition of text

      1. Allows for more importance placed on the music

      2. No need for concern that a thick, contrapuntal texture will cover the words

      3. Allows for a higher degree of rhythmic activity than in normal speech

       4.   Expands the melodic line beyond the scope of the poetic phrase

  D. The opposite is true when the text is needed to tell a story or describe dialogue

       1.   In Baroque and Classical opera recitative, the words dictate the rhythm

       2.   Very little text repetition

  E. Thick musical textures present another consideration for the composer

  F. Opera composers deal with many different elements when setting text to music

       1.   Explain actions

       2.   Describe events

       3.   Establish dialogue

       4.   Express a variety of emotions

  G. Verdi (see Chapter 9)

       1.   Worked with a librettist who was himself a composer: Arrigo Boïto

       2.   Felt strongly about the need to support and interpret the words without dominating them

       3.   Orchestrations maintained a sense of clarity and brilliance

  H. Wagner (see Chapter 9)

       1.   Wrote his own libretto

       2.   Relied heavily on the emotional power of the orchestra

       3.   Used instrumental sections to expound on the emotions drawn from the text

IV. Giacomo Puccini and Alban Berg (pp. 233-241)

  A. These two composers offer contrasting operatic styles

       1.   A difference in compositional techniques

           a.   Puccini writes very tonal music in the tradition of Mozart and Verdi

           b.   Berg uses atonal and expressionist techniques

       2.   Subject matter is very different

           a.   Puccini sets a simple love story in which reality is blurred by romance

           b.   Berg sets a depressing story of frustrated love and life

       3.   Both composers are highly effective in composing dramatic music

  B. GIACOMO PUCCINI (see biography, p. 234)

       1.   Wrote several operas between 1883 and his death in 1924

       2.   Focused on VERISMO (realism) in his works

           a.   Operas depicted realistic situations, ordinary people

           b.   Style incorporates a wide range of emotions

       3.   Puccini typically wrote powerful melodies and themes

           a.   With repetition the themes identify characters or situations to the audience

           b.   Modified themes reflect changes in the plot

       4.   LISTENING NOTES: *La Bohème*, end of Act I (pp. 235-237)

C. ALBAN BERG (see biography, p. 238)

   1. Berg's opera *Wozzeck* is considered the most significant expressionist opera written

   2. The entire work is organized according to traditional forms

      a. Consists of three acts

         i. Act I--Exposition

         ii. Act II--Development

         iii. Act III--Catastrophe

      b. Each act consists of five scenes structured like single movements of an instrumental piece

         i. Act II has five scenes that are structured like movements of a symphony

            1. Sonata-allegro

            2. Fantasia and fugue

            3. Largo

            4. Scherzo

            5. Rondo

         ii. The five scenes in Act III are a series of variations

            1. Variations on a theme

            2. Variations on a single tone

            3. Variations on a rhythmic pattern

            4. Variations on a chord

            5. Variations on continuous running notes

      c. This sense of organization and structure is part of the expressionist thinking of serial composers

      d. Organization may also reflect an effort to restore order after the abandonment of tonality

   3. Based on a play written in the early 1830s, but a very contemporary plot

   4. Words and music balance beautifully in a tragic and cynical work

   5. Plot is simple but powerful

   6. Range of emotion is phenomenal

      a. Expressionistic emotions

         i. Despair

         ii. Frustration

         iii. Uselessness

         iv. Lack of worth

      b. Traditional emotions

         i. Love

    ii. Yearning

    iii. Anger

    iv. Hate

  7. Dialogue and settings are realistic

  8. Music is dissonant and contorted

  9. Opera and music found a new balance in this opera

  10. LISTENING NOTES: *Wozzeck*, Act III, Scenes 4 and 5 (pp. 239-241)

 V. Words as Music (pp. 241-242)

  A. Words and their sounds have been explored by both poets and composers in the 20th century

  B. Hans Helms, *FA:M'ANIESGEWOW*

   1. Uses sounds common to both English and Russian

   2. Uses a technique called synthetic polyglot and verbal polyphony

  C. Kurt Schwitters, *Sonate*

   1. The sound of the words and syllables create the music: SOUND POETRY

    a. Writing words and/or syllables for their sound alone

    b. The meaning of the text may be irrelevant

   2. Rhythm and pitch are a product of the recitation

   3. See text, p. 242

  D. Music and words are forever intertwined and the perception of the artist and performer will resolve the tensions between the two

EXERCISES

1. Listen to the motet *Absalon fili mi* by Josquin Desprez. How does the voice range of this motet compare to the range of other works by Josquin, such as the motet studied in Chapter 6 (*Ave Christie Immolate*). Does Josquin use the word painting technique in *Absalon*? If so, how is the technique used? What words are emphasized and how are they emphasized in the music? How does the word painting in this example compare to the word painting in other motets and in madrigals?

2. Listen to sections 5 through 9 of Handel's oratorio *Israel in Egypt*. As the voices are telling about the plagues sent to Egypt, how are these plagues portrayed in the music? Are the plagues musically described by just the voices? By just the orchestra? Or are they musically described by both the chorus and the orchestra? Do these musical descriptions help you to imagine the various plagues? Is there any incidences of imitation used in the choruses? If so, do the words remain clear enough to understand what is going on or is the texture very confusing?

3. Listen to *Come Out* by Steve Reich. In this piece for taped voice, how does the composer use the voice to create rhythmic patterns? How is the tape manipulated to help create this effect? Can the rhythmic pattern be organized into a specific meter? Why or why not? Do you think other phrases could be incorporated into the mix of this piece to expand the work? Make up a phrase that you think could serve as a countersubject to Reich's "Come out and show them."

STUDY QUESTIONS

1. One of the most important arguments in music is whether music should be subservient or equal to the words. (p. 228)
   A. True
   B. False

2. In early chant, words were set to a single melody called (p. 228)
   A. Homophony
   B. Polyphony
   C. Monophony
   D. Heterophony

3. The melodic device that placed several notes on one text syllable is called (p. 228)
   A. A melissa
   B. A melisma
   C. A miasma
   D. A magma

4. The above named device was used to _____ a specific word or idea. (p. 228)

5. A borrowed melody from a chant that was used as the basis of a polyphonic composition is called _____ _____. (p. 228)

6. This borrowed melody is found in the _____ or lowest part of a song. (p. 228)

7. The borrowed melody was slowed to a drone. (p. 228)
   A. True
   B. False

8. The upper voices in these motets moved at a slower pace than the lowest voice. (p. 228)
   A. True
   B. False

9. The thick texture of these motets represent a move toward (p. 229)

   _____

10. A secular love poem set to music that was popular in the Renaissance is the (p. 229)

    A.   Madrigal

    B.   Motet

    C.   Mass

    D.   Miserere

11. Jannequin's _____ are clear examples of his attempt to imitate the meaning
    of the words with music. (p. 229)

12. The practice of stressing a certain word musically is called _____ _____. (p. 229)

13. The place at which a new text phrase begins and each voice part enters in turn using the same
    melodic idea is called (p. 229)

    A.   The cadence

    B.   Word painting

    C.   A madrigalism

    D.   Points of imitation

14. The end of large or small musical ideas is called (p. 229)

    A.   The cadence

    B.   Word painting

    C.   A madrigalism

    D.   Points of imitation

15. A motet is a secular choral work that is set polyphonically. (p. 229)

    A.   True

    B.   False

16. Sacred music was redirected toward a more conservative texture by (p. 230)

    A.   The Council of Versailles

    B.   The Council of Trent

    C.   The Council of Nicaea

    D.   The Council of Avignon

17. In the Baroque period, a new style of singing called _____ was established. (p. 230)

18. This singing style was a more even balance between music and the text. (p. 230)

    A.   True

    B.   False

19. This style of singing was developed by (p. 230)

    A.   The Viennese Orchestra

    B.   The Russian Five

    C.   The Roman Opera Directors

    D.   The Florentine Camerata

20. The group named in question 19 consisted of intellectual _____ and _____. (p. 230)

21. The work of this group successfully eliminated the use of polyphony in the Baroque. (p. 230)

    A.   True

    B.   False

22. A major concern of Romantic composers such as Schubert and Schumann was (p. 231)

    _____

23. The vocal technique used by Schoenberg in *Pierrot Lunaire* is called _____. (p. 231)

24. In which of the following popular music styles is the music more important than the words? (p. 231)

    A.   Country & western

    B.   Rap

    C.   Commercial dance

    D.   Romantic ballads

25. The most important concern for a composer in choosing a text is _____ _____. (p. 231)

26. The person who transforms the words into patterns of rhythms and sounds to stimulate the composer is called (p. 231)

    A.   The librettist

    B.   The poet

    C.   The bookmaker

    D.   The wordsmith

27. The sound of a word can affect the tone and texture of a composition. (p. 231)

    A.   True

    B.   False

28. When text repetition is present in the libretto, (p. 232)

    A.   The audience becomes bored

    B.   The music takes precedence over the words

    C.   The orchestra can play louder

    D.   The words take precedence over the music

29. Repetition allows for a higher degree of _____ activity than in normal speech. (p. 232)

30. Repetition expands the melodic line beyond the scope of the poetic phrase. (p. 232)

    A.   True

    B.   False

31. The musical element in Baroque and Classical opera that is used to tell the story is called (p. 232)

    A.   Aria

    B.   Monody

    C.   Libretto

    D.   Recitative

32. In the technique named in question 31, the level of repetition is _____. (p. 232)

33. The musical element in Baroque and Classical opera that is expressive and used to comment on an emotion is called (p. 232)

    A.   Aria

    B.   Monody

    C.   Libretto

    D.   Recitative

34. Singing styles make understanding one's own language easier. (p. 232)

    A.   True

    B.   False

35. Which of the following is NOT true of Verdi? (p. 232)

    A.   His orchestrations maintained a sense of clarity

    B.   He felt the words should be supported by the music

    C.   He relied on the emotional power of the orchestra to overpower the words

    D.   He worked with a librettist who was also a good opera composer

36. Puccini's operas are (p. 233)

    A.   Atonal and in Italian

    B.   Tonal and in German

    C.   Atonal and in German

    D.   Tonal and in Italian

37. Berg's operas are (p. 233)

    A.   Atonal and in Italian

    B.   Tonal and in German

    C.   Atonal and in German

    D.   Tonal and in Italian

38. Berg is from the school of (p. 233)

    A.   German expressionism

    B.   Italian verismo

    C.   German verismo

    D.   Italian expressionism

39. Powerful melodies or themes are _____ when repeated immediately (p. 237)

40. Powerful melodies are also a source of character identity and _____. (p. 237)

41. The opera *Wozzeck* is organized according to traditional forms. (p. 237)

    A.   True

    B.   False

42. Berg refers to the three acts of *Wozzeck* as (p. 237)

    A.   Exposition, Development, and Recapitulation

    B.   Exposition, Episode, and Fugue

    C.   Exposition, Development, and Catastrophe

    D.   Exposition, Development, and Epilogue

43. The second act is made up of scenes that are structured like single movements of

    _____. (p. 237)

44. The scenes of the third act are a series of _____. (p. 237)

45. The extreme organization of *Wozzeck* can be seen as an effort to restore order when _____

    was abandoned. (p. 238)

46. The libretto of *Wozzeck* offers great latitude for setting dialogue and _____

    development. (p. 238)

47. The opera *Wozzeck* eventually has a happy ending. (p. 241)

    A.   True

    B.   False

48. The dialogue and settings are realistic and the music is (p. 241)

    A.   Loud and consonant

    B.   Dissonant and contorted

    C.   Primarily tonal

    D.   Consonant and eclectic

49. The technique in which meaningful words in one language can be heard while a text in another

    language is recited is known as synthetic polyglot and _____ _____. (p. 241)

50. The technique in which the sound of words and syllables create music is called (p. 241)

    A.   Verbal sparring

    B.   Word of mouth

    C.   Stream of consciousness

    D.   Sound poetry

51. In the above named technique, the meaning of the text is highly important to the performance.

    (p. 241)

    A.   True

    B.   False

52. Music and words will be forever intertwined. (p. 241)

    A.   True

    B.   False

TOPIC 4, THE CONDUCTOR AND COMPOSITION

I. Introduction (p. 243)

    A. Conductors are generally considered to be an important part of any performance involving a large musical group

    B. The need for conductors came about over a period of time

        1. Earlier music had very little changes in tempo or dynamics

        2. In the Baroque period, TERRACED DYNAMICS were sudden increases and decreases

            a. When loud dynamics were needed, composers wrote for more instruments

            b. Soft sounds were written for smaller numbers of players

    C. It is unknown whether conductors led to new musical styles or new musical styles required more direction and more conductors

    D. As musical styles developed so did conducting techniques

II. The Development of Conducting Techniques (pp. 243-245)

    A. The need for organization became more important as the size of performing groups grew

    B. The first recorded method of conducting can be traced to the 15th century

        1. Chief singer of the Sistine Chapel choir beat time for the other singers

        2. The basic beat was called the TAKTUS

        3. Used a rolled up paper to beat time

        4. Method was probably used for difficult passages in which singers had difficulty staying together

    C. The art of conducting was not firmly established in early periods because the number of musicians used in performances was not very large

    D. Eventually the roll of paper gave way to a large stick of cane to beat time

    E. By the 18th century the leadership role moved to the harpsichordist

        1. Harpsichordist was often the composer

        2. The keyboard was used to steer the ensemble

    F. As the harpsichord was dropped from the ensemble, the leadership moved to the CONCERT MASTER

        1. Usually the first chair violin or the best violinist of the group

        2. Traditionally the assistant to the conductor

        3. The concert master would move his or her bow up and down to bring the players together

        4. In modern orchestras this player enters last before the conductor and tunes the group

    G. An important change in conducting occurred with Mendelssohn in the 19th century

        1. Helped define the conductor as an interpreter of music

        2. Placed the conductor at a music stand in front of the orchestra

3. Used a stick (BATON) to conduct the group

4. Tempo and dynamic changes could be seen by the performers and by the audience

H. Levels of volume are determined by the conductor's interpretation of what is most musically correct

I. Wagner is considered the first modern conductor

1. Insisted on controlling every facet of a performance

2. His control was greater than most conductors because he was conducting his own music

3. Rehearsed musicians so that melody was never lost and tempo was always correct

J. By the late 19th century, the role of the conductor had been determined

III. Style of Conducting (p. 245)

A. Conducting patterns (see Chapter 4) are used to indicate the location of each beat in a measure

B. Strict beat patterns are not necessary with well-trained musicians

1. Conductor may use more expressive body movements

2. Some conductors have abandoned beat motions in favor of outlining the development of phrases and dynamics

3. These conductors are more concerned with larger musical elements than with momentary rhythmic activities

C. Small chamber groups do not use conductors

1. Performers respond to one another based on decisions made in rehearsals

2. Small body motions unify the ensemble stylistically and rhythmically

IV. Responsibilities of the Conductor (pp. 245-248)

A. The role of the conductor as interpreter was not universally accepted

1. Must the conductor accurately represent the intent of the composer?

2. How much of a performance should be a conductor's personal interpretation?

3. Which is more important, the composer's original ideas or the conductor's interpretation?

B. Various solutions to these questions have yielded different performances of the same works over the last two hundred years

C. Preparation for conducting is very extensive

1. Conductors must analyze a great deal of music

2. Conductors must also study rehearsal techniques to make the most of rehearsal time

3. Some conductors do the most work at rehearsal so that the orchestra knows in advance what is expected in performance

4. Some conductors make last minute decisions to make the music responsive to the moment

D. Some conductors specialize in the works of specific composers

E. All conductors must exhibit a knowledge of the standard repertoire but often show a greater intensity when conducting works in which they have specialized

F. Many listeners have not only favorite works but favorite conductors of those works

G. The job of the conductor has grown in importance beyond rehearsal and performance

    1. The conductor is the visual representation of what is happening and what will happen

    2. The conductor gives a CUE to a performer for the next required musical effect

    3. Great conductors are tour guides for the audience

    4. The communication of musical ideas is a three-way experience

        a. Conductor

        b. Performers

        c. Audience

    5. The popularity of successful conductors hinges on their ability to excite the audience as well as the orchestra

H. The personality of the conductor helps to build symphony organizations

    1. The conductor's primary concern is to program interesting music

    2. Successful conductors can manipulate the musical arena as well as support activities

V. Orchestral Musicians (pp. 248-250)

A. Conductors are not always able to get the musical interpretations they want from the musicians under their direction

    1. The conductor must choose literature that is within the abilities of the musicians

    2. Tempo considerations must be evaluated for each performing group

    3. Musicians are critical tools in the building of a performance

B. Musicians in professional orchestras are very well prepared

    1. Musicians are required to play different selections in a variety of musical styles

    2. They practice parts from EXCERPT BOOKS, difficult or soloistic parts from the standard orchestral literature

    3. Performers are aware of stylistic differences between Mozart and Mahler, or early and late Beethoven for example

C. Conductors and musicians rehearse to create a team unified by the conductor's interpretation

D. Orchestral musicians play from one notated part and must be able to weave their part into the fabric of the whole

    1. Musicians must know what motives or themes on which to place emphasis

    2. The conductor helps the musicians interpret the music

E. The orchestral musician's ability to blend with the other musicians is critical

    1. They must listen to other musicians around them

    2. They must be responsive to the conductor

    3. They must be able to place their sound into the total musical image

EXERCISES

The best exercise to understand the role of the conductor or leader of a musical group is to attend rehearsals and performances of different types of musical groups, including large symphony orchestras, chamber ensembles such as string quartets or quintets, jazz big bands, symphonic bands, small jazz combos, and even small rock groups. Attend at least three rehearsals and one performance by any two of the groups listed here or similar groups. Take note of the techniques used in rehearsing the music that is to be played and keep a rehearsal log of how much time is spent in rehearsal. Ask yourself how the time is spent in rehearsal, whether it is spent working on interpretation or whether it is spent just learning the notes. Which rehearsals are more beneficial to the ultimate production of the music in performance? Is rehearsal time more effective when there is at least one leader and the musicians listen to and respond to that leader? Write up your findings in a brief essay.

STUDY QUESTIONS

1. Conductors were not required in early music periods. (p. 243)

   A.   True

   B.   False

2. Composers originally wrote music that required (p. 243)

   A.   Wide ranges in dynamic levels

   B.   Wide variances of tempo

   C.   Few changes in dynamics

   D.   A strong need for leadership

3. An example of dynamic change in the Baroque was called _____ _____. (p. 243)

4. In this style of dynamics, change occurred gradually and subtly. (p. 243)

   A.   True

   B.   False

5. In the Baroque when loud volumes were necessary, composers wrote (p. 243)

   A.   For more musicians

   B.   For brass and percussion instruments

   C.   For strings and brass instruments

   D.   For smaller groups of musicians

6. A gradual increase in volume is called _____. (p. 243)

7. A gradual decrease in volume is called _____ (p. 243)

8. The need for organization increased as performing groups (p. 243)

    A.   Became more virtuosic

    B.   Grew in size

    C.   Charged more for tickets

    D.   Played more frequently

9. The first recorded method of conducting can be traced back to (p. 243)

    A.   The 18th century

    B.   The 16th century

    C.   The 15th century

    D.   The 12th century

10. In early music, the beat was referred to as the _____. (p 244)

11. Simple time beating was probably used when musicians had a difficult time staying together. (p. 244)

    A.   True

    B.   False

12. By the 1700s the leadership role of a musical group had fallen to (p. 244)

    A.   The first violinist

    B.   The timpanist

    C.   The first trumpet

    D.   The harpsichordist

13. The performer who played the instrument named above was also often the composer. (p. 244)

    A.   True

    B.   False

14. As ensembles grew in size, which of the following instruments was dropped from the orchestra?

    (p. 244)

    A.   The clarinet

    B.   The harpsichord

    C.   The first violin

    D.   The trumpet

15. The person who is the assistant to the conductor is called the _____ _____. (p. 244)

16. This person is traditionally (p. 244)

    A.   The first violinist

    B.   The timpanist

    C.   The first trumpet

    D.   The harpsichordist

17. When the ensemble needed direction, the person named in question 16 would

    A.   Beat time loudly on the timpani

    B.   Play loud chords on the harpsichord

    C.   Move the violin bow up and down with the beat

    D.   Play a loud fanfare on the trumpet

18. The composer who helped define the role of the conductor in the 19th century was (p. 244)

    A.   Robert Schumann

    B.   Gustav Mahler

    C.   Franz Liszt

    D.   Felix Mendelssohn

19. This style of conducting placed the conductor (p. 244)

    A.   At the piano

    B.   In front of the orchestra

    C.   To the side of the orchestra

    D.   In the percussion section

20. The conductor led the orchestra with a _____. (p. 244)

21. Tempo and dynamic changes could not be clearly seen by the performers or the audience. (p. 245)

    A.   True

    B.   False

22. Levels of volume are determined by the conductor's personal _____ of what is most musically correct. (p. 245)

23. The composer often referred to as the first modern conductor was (p. 245)

    A.   Franz Liszt

    B.   Richard Wagner

    C.   Richard Strauss

    D.   Ludwig van Beethoven

24. The composer above wanted to control all aspects of performance from rehearsal to concert. (p. 245)

    A.   True

    B.   False

25. This composer rehearsed the musicians so that the _____ was never lost and the _____ was always correct. (p. 245)

26. Conducting patterns are used to indicate (p. 245)

    A.   The tempo of a piece

    B.   Key changes within a piece

    C.   The location of each beat in a measure

    D.   The beginning of each movement

27. Some conductors abandon conducting patterns and move with body motions that elicit higher levels of _____. (p. 245)

28. These conductors are concerned with (p. 245)

    A. Larger musical elements

    B. Keeping track of the beats

    C. What instrument is playing the theme

    D. Keeping track of the tempo

29. Small chamber groups respond to each other in light of decisions made at rehearsals. (p. 245)

    A. True

    B. False

30. In performance, chamber performers use small body motions to unify the ensemble _____ and rhythmically. (p. 245)

31. The role of the conductor as interpreter is universally accepted. (p. 245)

    A. True

    B. False

32. Why must a conductor analyze music and study rehearsal techniques? (p. 247)

    _____

33. Why do some conductors specialize in the works of specific composers? (p. 247)

    _____

34. The conductor is the _____ _____ of what is happening in the music (p. 248)

35. The visual motion made by the conductor to instruct a performer of an entrance is called (p. 248)

    A. A "nod"

    B. "Pointing"

    C. A "cue"

    D. A "fare attenzione"

36. Great conductors are tour guides for the audience. (p. 248)

    A. True

    B. False

37. The communication of musical ideas is a three-way experience between _____, _____, and _____. (p. 248)

38. The popularity of many successful conductors hinges on (p. 248)

    A. Their ability to choose good repertoire

    B. Their ability to excite the audience and the orchestra

    C. Their ability to hire good musicians

    D. Their ability to keep conducting even when they've lost their place

39. Conductors are often required to organize fundraising projects such as luncheons and banquets.
(p. 248)

    A.   True

    B.   False

40. The conductor's primary concern besides rehearsing and performing is to (p. 248)

    A.   Program interesting music

    B.   Attend luncheons and banquets

    C.   Organize auctions and charity events

    D.   Sell concert subscriptions

41. It is the responsibility of the conductor to choose music within the reach of the musicians. (p. 248)

    A.   True

    B.   False

42. Musicians are critical tools in building a _____ performance. (p. 249)

43. To prepare for orchestra auditions, musicians practice from books of orchestral passages called
_____ books. (p. 249)

44. The above named books contain excerpts from the standard orchestral literature that (p. 249)

    A.   Are easy to practice and learn

    B.   Are rarely used in actual concerts

    C.   Are especially difficult or soloistic

    D.   Emphasize one particular style period

45. The musicians and conductor rehearse in order to create a team that is unified by the
_____ of the conductor. (p. 249)

46. Musicians in an orchestra see only one notated part and must exhibit the ability to weave their
part into the whole. (p. 249)

    A.   True

    B.   False

47. The musicians, with the help of the conductor, must be able to (p. 249)

    A.   Read the music correctly

    B.   Place emphasis on important melodies and rhythms

    C.   Find the tonal center

    D.   Organize rehearsals

48. The musician's ability to blend what they play with other sounds around them is critical. (p. 249)

    A.   True

    B.   False

TOPIC 5, THE INSTRUMENTAL SOLOIST

I. The Soloist and the Orchestra (pp. 251-257)

    A. The premier form for virtuoso display is the CONCERTO

        1. The first secular concert work called a concerto is attributed to Torelli (1686)

        2. The form was adopted and developed by Corelli and Vivaldi (see Chapter 7)

    B. The CONCERTO GROSSO was an important instrumental form in the Baroque period

        1. A small ensemble is contrasted against the large orchestra

        2. The soloists exhibit virtuosic displays of performance

        3. Part of the drama of the piece occurs in the contrasting dynamic levels of the two groups

        4. Also pits contrasting tone colors against a full orchestral backdrop

        5. Examples:

            a. Vivaldi, *The Four Seasons* (four concerti grossi)

            b. Bach, *The Brandenburg Concertos* (six concerti grossi)

    C. The Classical concerto

        1. Retained the three-movement structure of the concerto grosso

        2. Featured one soloist rather than a group of soloists

        3. The composers were great soloists and these concerti were written for themselves

            a. Mozart

            b. Beethoven

        4. These composers' mastery of the form set the standard for others to follow

        5. These composers were also well known for their ability to improvise a CADENZA

            a. Unaccompanied solo that is very free rhythmically and melodically

            b. Generally appears in the first movement, and sometimes the last movement, of a solo concerto

            c. Traditionally follows a relatively dissonant chord in the orchestra

            d. Soloist plays exciting technical displays of his or her skills

            e. Often develops material presented earlier in the movement

            f. The soloist signal the end of the cadenza traditionally with a long trill

            g. The orchestra, which has been silent during the cadenza, resolves the earlier dissonant chord

        6. Form

            a. Consists of three movements; the third, or dance, movement typical of the symphony is deleted in the concerto

            b. The first movement generally follows the sonata-allegro form

            c. Middle movement is slower and contrasting

  d. The favored form of the third movement is rondo form

  e. There are of course exceptions to the standard structure

 D. Important changes occurred in the concerto from the Classical to the Romantic periods

  1. Those of Haydn and Mozart had three distinct movements

  2. The works of Mozart and Haydn helped define the concerto

  3. The concertos of Beethoven introduce a shift in priorities

   a. The orchestra became a more dominant force

   b. The balance between solo virtuosity and orchestral power intensified the drama

   c. Romantic concertos became large, emotionally-charged structures

  4. In Mendelssohn's *Violin Concerto*, the three movements are smoothly connected without stopping

  5. In Liszt's piano concertos, the movements are connected without stopping and also share thematic material

 E. The piano was a favored instrument for concertos but other solo instruments intrigued composers as well

  1. LISTENING NOTES: Haydn, *Concerto for Trumpet in E-flat Major*, third movement (pp. 253-254)

   a. Written for a friend who invented a keyed trumpet

   b. One of the first concertos for modern trumpet

  2. LISTENING NOTES: FELIX MENDELSSOHN (see biography, p. 255), *Violin Concerto in E Minor, Op. 64*, first movement (pp. 256-257)

   a. Also composed for a friend

   b. Illustrates Mendelssohn's thorough knowledge and understanding of the violin

II. Full Circle (pp. 257-260)

 A. The concerto exhibited a great deal of development in history

  1. The Baroque concerto grosso

  2. The Classical solo concerto

  3. A return to the Baroque orchestral concerto in the 20th century

   a. Bartok, *Concerto for Orchestra*

   b. Considered a concerto because of the soloistic nature of the instruments

 B. Modern concertos continue to experiment with different combinations of soloists and orchestra

  1. Arthur Bliss, *Concerto for Piano, Tenor, Xylophone, and Strings*

  2. LISTENING NOTES: ELLEN TAAFE ZWILICH (see biography, p. 258), *Concerto Grosso 1985*, first movement (p. 259)

   a. No specific soloist, an orchestral concerto

   b. Consists of five movements

   c. Principal theme is based on a theme from Handel's *Violin Sonata in D Major*

  3. Zwilich, *Concerto for Trumpet and Five Players*

   a. Further evidence of the flexibility of the modern concerto

   b. The solo trumpet is accompanied by a wide range of tone colors and textures

   c. Returns to the three-movement structure of the Classical and Romantic concertos

   d. The orchestra is replaced by a chamber ensemble

  4. Elliott Carter, *Piano Concerto*

   a. Introduces three contrasting elements

    i. The solo piano

    ii. The orchestra

    iii. A CONCERTINO group of seven instruments

   b. The concertino group acts as an intermediary between the piano and the orchestra

   c. Raises contrast to another level of complexity and intellectualism

 C. The term "concerto" continues to reappear as new forms in which contrasting musical ideas and sounds are composed

III. The Soloist in Chamber Music (pp. 260-262)

 A. The SONATA is a genre for soloist but in an intimate, chamber setting rather than a concert setting, as was the concerto

 B. The term originally meant music that was to be played (instrumental music) as opposed to music that was sung (vocal music)

 C. The Baroque sonata

  1. Dominated by sonatas for violin

  2. Eventually developed into the TRIO SONATA

   a. A sonata with three musical parts

   b. The two upper parts are played by soloists

   c. The bass line is played by a BASSO CONTINUO

    i. A figured bass played by a chording instrument (keyboard, lute)

    ii. Bass line is reinforced by another bass instrument (cello)

 D. The sonata eventually evolved into a three-movement work similar to the concerto

  1. Accompaniment was by basso continuo rather than orchestra

  2. Exceptions were sonatas for keyboard instruments

  3. There are also brilliant examples of solo instrument sonatas with no accompaniment

 E. The Classical sonata

  1. Borrowed the structure of the multimovement keyboard suites of the Baroque

  2. Eventually settled on three movements

  3. The dance third movement was deleted by the end of the 18th century

4. The construction of the piano improved in the 19th century

   a. Resulted in more brilliance and sound projection

   b. Particularly interested the composers who themselves played the piano

5. LISTENING NOTES: Beethoven, *Piano Sonata in F Minor, Op. 57*, first movement (pp. 261-262)

EXERCISES

1. Listen to the *Concerto in C Major for Mandolin and Strings* by Antonio Vivaldi. What is the overall structure of this piece? How many movements are there? What is the form of each movement? Can you follow the form of the first and last movements as you listen to this piece? Listen especially close to the first movement of this piece. Create a graphic diagram or map of this movement that shows where the soloist plays and where the orchestra plays. When the soloist plays, is it just the soloist that is playing or are there other instruments that support the soloist?

2. Listen to *Sonata in G Minor for Solo Violin*, BWV 1001 by J. S. Bach. This sonata is in the "sonata da chiesa" format; what is meant by this? (See Chapter 7.) This is also an example of solo sonata that has no other instrument accompanying the violin, not even the basso continuo. How does Bach create the illusion of a solo melodic line accompanied by a supporting instrument? Is this an effective style of composition? Does it sound as if there is more than one instrument playing at times? How does tempo contribute to the overall perception of this piece? What else can you say about this piece?

3. Listen to *Piano Concerto No. 5 in E-flat Major, Op. 73* by Beethoven. Compared with other piano concertos by Beethoven and Mozart, how does Beethoven's "Emperor Concerto" balance between the soloist and the orchestra? Is this concerto similar in stature to the Fifth Symphony? Why or why not? Into which of Beethoven's creative periods does this concerto fit? What style characteristics are present in this concerto that tie it to that particular creative period?

4. Listen to *Sonata in B Minor* by Franz Liszt. Discuss the form of this sonata. How many movements are there in this work? Can the piece be perceived as sectional? If so, how does Liszt achieve this sectionalization? How is tempo used to create a feeling of sectionalization? Mode or harmony? Are there any other divisive elements present in this work? How does Liszt use texture in this piece? Is there a feeling at any time in this piece that there seems to be more than one instrument playing at one time? If so, how is this achieved? What else can be said about this piece?

STUDY QUESTIONS

1. The premier form for virtuoso display is (p. 251)

   A. The sonata

   B. The symphony

   C. The concerto

   D. The suite

2. The first secular concert work called a concerto is attributed to (p. 251)

   A. Corelli

   B. Torelli

   C. Bach

   D. Vivaldi

3. The two composers who adopted and developed the concerto were _____ and _____. (p. 251)

4. The earliest concertos featured several soloists of a small ensemble within the orchestra. (p. 251)

   A. True

   B. False

5. The type of concerto in which a group of soloists is contrasted against the full orchestra is called a _____ _____. (p. 251)

6. Perhaps the most famous of this type of concerto are the six Brandenburg concertos by (p. 251)

   A. Corelli

   B. Torelli

   C. Bach

   D. Vivaldi

7. The number of movements in the typical Classical concerto are (p. 252)

   A. Four

   B. Six

   C. Five

   D. Three

8. The Classical concerto typically features a group of soloists. (p. 252)

   A. True

   B. False

9. Classical concerto composers were often brilliant soloists themselves. (p. 252)

   A. True

   B. False

10. The improvised solo that is somewhat free in rhythm and meter is called _____. (p. 252)

11. Which of the following is NOT true of the cadenza? (p. 252)

    A.   The soloist displays a great deal of technical skill

    B.   The orchestra accompanies the soloist softly until the soloist is finished

    C.   The soloist usually develops thematic material from earlier in the movement

    D.   The cadenza generally appears in the first movement of a concerto

12. The soloist customarily signals the end of the solo with (p. 252)

    A.   A long trill

    B.   A short tonic chord arpeggio

    C.   A pounding of tonic and dominant chords

    D.   A shout of "Bring it on home"

13. Which movement of the typical symphony plan was deleted to make the typical concerto

    three movements? (p. 252)

    A.   The finale

    B.   The scherzo

    C.   The opening allegro

    D.   The slow movement

14. The first movement of a concerto generally follows _____ form. (p. 252)

15. The second movement of the concerto is usually _____ in tempo. (p. 252)

16. The favorite structure for the last movement of the concerto is (p. 252)

    A.   Sonata-allegro

    B.   Scherzo and trio

    C.   Rondo

    D.   Theme and variations

17. The favored solo instrument in the Classical period for the concerto was the _____. (p. 252)

18. Haydn's *Concerto in E-flat Major* was one of the first concertos for the modern _____.

    (p. 252)

19. Which two composers helped define the Classical solo concerto? (p. 254)

    A.   _____

    B.   _____

20. In the concertos of Beethoven, the _____ became a more dominant force. (p. 254)

21. Which of the following helped the Romantic concerto become a large, emotionally-charged form?

    (p. 254)

    A.   Using groups of solo instruments

    B.   Relying on simple tonic/dominant harmonies

    C.   The increased size of the orchestra

    D.   Smaller orchestral sections

22. In Mendelssohn's *Concerto in E Minor* the movements (p. 252)

    A.   Are smoothly connected without stopping

    B.   Share thematic material

    C.   Are clearly divided into three movements

    D.   Are clearly divided into four movements

23. Mendelssohn's *Concerto in E Minor* supposedly sounds easy but is difficult to play. (p. 254)

    A.   True

    B.   False

24. In the first movement of Mendelssohn's *Concerto in E Minor*, the cadenza (p. 256)

    A.   Occurs at the end of the movement

    B.   Introduces the exposition

    C.   Occurs between the exposition and the development

    D.   Occurs between the development and the recapitulation

25. The cadenza in Mendelssohn's *Concerto in E Minor* is improvised by the soloist. (p. 256)

    A.   True

    B.   False

26. Bartók's *Concerto for Orchestra* is an example of (p. 257)

    A.   Solo concerto

    B.   Orchestral concerto

    C.   Concerto grosso

    D.   Concerto obligatto

27. Modern concertos composers experiment with _____ _____ of soloists and orchestra. (p. 257)

28. Ellen Zwilich's *Concerto Grosso 1985* is based on a theme by (p. 257)

    A.   Vivaldi

    B.   Bach

    C.   Mozart

    D.   Handel

29. Zwilich's *Concerto Grosso 1985* is written in the spirit of the (p. 257)

    A.   Solo concerto

    B.   Orchestral concerto

    C.   Concerto grosso

    D.   Concerto obligatto

30. The use of the _____ in this work gives the music a nostalgic link with the Baroque period. (p. 259)

31. Zwilich was awarded the _____ in 1983, the first granted to a woman in the field of music composition. (p. 258)

    A.   Pulitzer Prize

    B.   Academy Award

    C.   Grammy Award

    D.   Nobel Prize

32. Zwilich's *Concerto for Trumpet and Five Players* is unusual in that (p. 260)

    A.   The work is in three movements

    B.   It features a solo trumpet

    C.   The orchestra is replaced by a chamber ensemble

    D.   There is a part for solo tenor voice

33. Elliott Carter's *Piano Concerto* uses three contrasting elements: the soloist, the orchestra, and a _____ _____. (p. 260)

34. The term _____ reappears throughout music history to indicate forms that feature contrasting musical ideas and sounds. (p. 260)

35. The parallel structure for soloists in chamber music is the _____. (p. 260)

36. Before the Baroque period, the term "sonata" meant (p. 260)

    A.   Music for the chamber

    B.   Music to be played

    C.   Music to be sung

    D.   Music for the church

37. _____ sonatas were the first to dominate the musical world. (p. 260)

38. The trio sonata has (p. 260)

    A.   Three musical parts for four players

    B.   Two musical parts for three players

    C.   Three musical parts for three players

    D.   Four musical parts for three players

39. The performance of a figured bass by a chording instrument and reinforced by a bass instrument is called (p. 260)

    A.   Basso ostinato

    B.   Basso obligatto

    C.   Basso constanto

    D.   Basso continuo

40. The sonata typically has _____ movements. (p. 260)

41. The primary difference between the sonata and the concerto is that the sonata accompaniment is provided by _____. (p. 260)

42. The exception to the type of sonata named in question 41 were sonatas for (p. 260)

    A.   Flute

    B.   Keyboards

    C.   Violin

    D.   Clarinet

43. Why are sonatas for the above named instruments exceptions? (p. 260)

    _____

44. From what Baroque genre did piano sonatas borrow their structure? (p. 260)

    _____

45. The _____ of the piano was improved in the 19th century to provide more brilliance and projection. (p. 261)

46. In Beethoven's *Piano Sonata in F Minor, Op. 57*, there is no break between the second and last movements. (p. 261)

    A.   True

    B.   False

47. In what way is the first movement of Beethoven's *Piano Sonata in F Minor, Op. 57* similar to the first movement of his *Symphony No. 5 in C Minor*? (p. 261)

    _____

TOPIC 6, STRING QUARTETS

I. Introduction (p. 263)

    A. Chamber ensembles

        1. Small groups of musicians

        2. Perform in intimate settings

        3. Size ranges from one soloist to a small orchestra of fifteen to twenty players

        4. Concert music for small rooms

    B. The string quartet has been a favorite format for composers since the late 1700s

        1. Two violins play the treble range

        2. One viola that plays the alto range

        3. One cello that plays the tenor and bass ranges

        4. Can produce unique soloistic sounds as well as lush blends of sound

        5. The character of the ensemble is the product of the composer's imagination

II. Historical Background (pp. 263-269)

    A. Haydn was one of the first composers to write for a string quartet

    B. The first quartets by Haydn were called DIVERTIMENTI

        1. A collection of dance-like forms

        2. Performed by small string ensembles

        3. The predecessors of the modern string quartet

    C. The quartet gradually replaced the Baroque TRIO SONATA in popularity

        1. Also consisted of four performers but three musical lines

        2. Two upper parts were played by treble soloists

        3. Lowest part was played by a basso continuo

        4. The quartet did not use a basso continuo

        5. There was a gradual equalization of the four parts

    D. The independence of each instrument took place slowly in the 18th century

        1. Haydn early quartets

            a. First violin part had more difficult passages

            b. Other parts played a more accompanimental role

            c. Carried on the homophonic tradition of the divertimenti

            d. Also took advantage of an exceptional musician playing the first violin part

        2. Later quartets emphasize more equality between the separate parts

            a. Resulted in a more unified texture

            b. Melodic lines were shared between parts

E. Haydn first showed tendencies of developmental writing in his quartets

    1. Developmental ideas were eventually expanded in his symphonies

    2. Developmental writing led to the formulation of sonata-allegro form

F. The string quartet had more subtle changes in tone quality than the orchestra

    1. Composers developed an arsenal of available sounds

        a. Pitch range

        b. Dynamic range

        c. PIZZICATO: plucked string sound

        d. ARCO: bowed string sound

        e. Several other highly developed articulations

G. The string quartet flowered under Haydn's guidance

    1. Established a well-defined identity for others to imitate

    2. Other composers developed the string quartet over the next two hundred years

    3. LISTENING NOTES: *String Quartet in E-flat, Op. 33, No. 2*, ("The Joke"), fourth movement (pp. 264-265)

H. The classical string quartet reached a high point with Beethoven at the beginning of the 19th century

    1. Late quartets are profound and weighty works

    2. Beethoven's mature style is evident in his last five quartets and a fugue

    3. Some consider these quartets to be the most intellectual writing of Beethoven's career

    4. All were written during his third creative period

    5. Represent a firm footing in the Romantic style

    6. Demand aggressive virtuosity from the players

    7. Rich, full sonorities are produced in all four parts

    8. LISTENING NOTES: *String Quartet in C-sharp Minor, Op. 131*, first movement (pp. 266-267)

I. The quartet in the Romantic period

    1. Composers include Schubert, Schumann, and Brahms

    2. Developed rich sonorities

    3. Increased levels of dissonance and rhythmic complexity

    4. Articulations were expanded

        a. TREMOLO

            i. Vibrato motion of a pitch

            ii. Pitch moves slightly higher and lower

            iii. Adds more animation to the note

        b. DOUBLE-STOPS: playing two notes simultaneously

J. The string quartet in the 20th century

    1. Béla Bartók

        a. Reflect the durability of tonality and sonata-allegro form

        b. His six quartets push tonality to its extreme

        c. Melodies are very angular and powerful

        d. Extended performing techniques are more prevalent

        e. Evidence of the new virtuosity required of 20th-century performers

        f. LISTENING NOTES: *String Quartet No. 2, Op. 17*, second movement (pp. 267-269)

    2. Arnold Schoenberg

        a. Quartets use atonal sonorities

        b. Melodies are more angular

        c. Rhythms defy regular metric patterns

        d. Melodic ideas seem more rhythmic than tuneful

        e. Separate voices provide more intensity to these quartets

III. String Quartet in Transition (pp. 270-271)

    A. The string quartet has rarely found mass appeal because of their subtlety and refinement

    B. The flexibility and integrity of the string quartet has recently become evident in a more commercial setting

    C. Turtle Island String Quartet

        1. Comprised of four composer/arrangers

        2. Each has a solid background in traditional music

        3. Each has well-developed improvisation skills

        4. LISTENING NOTES: Darol Anger, *Street Stuff* (pp. 270-271)

    D. Contemporary composers look to the string quartet as a medium for experimentation and the development of musical thought

        1. Lejaren Hiller, *Iliac Suite*

            a. The first computer-generated composition (1957)

            b. Composed for string quartet

        2. Roger Reynolds, *Coconino: A Shattered Landscape for String Quartet*

            a. First developed through computer composition

            b. Eventually scored for string quartet

            c. Reynolds continues to use the string quartet as a vibrant medium for developing and expressing compositional thought

EXERCISES

1. Listen to the *Piano Quintet in A Major, Op. 114* by Franz Schubert. How does the overall form of this quintet compare with the overall form of Beethoven's late quartets? How does the instrumentation affect the perception of this quintet? Is the sound similar to Beethoven's late quartets in terms of texture? Harmony? Melody? Or is Schubert's approach to the chamber music genre quite different compared to Beethoven? Does the form of each movement seem to be based on traditional Classical forms or is there quite a bit of freedom in regards to structure?

2. Listen to the *String Quartet in F-sharp Minor, Op. 10* by Arnold Schoenberg. Is this piece effective as a crossover from Schoenberg's first style period to his second style period? Why or why not? How does the voice contribute to the overall perception of this quartet? How does the voice fit into the overall texture of this quartet? Does the text seem to have a special meaning within the context of this quartet? Does the tonal center of F-sharp minor remain constant throughout this piece? How do the forms of the first and second movements relate to other examples of string quartets, especially those from the late 19th century? In what way or ways are you affected by this quartet?

3. Listen to *Black Angels* by George Crumb. Describe as best you can the sounds that you are hearing in this piece for string quartet. Are the instruments used in a traditional manner or are they used in unconventional ways? How do the performers use different instrumental techniques to create a feeling of discomfort? Is there any sense of harmony present in this work? Does the composer use conventional forms? Describe your feelings about this piece. Is this the type of piece that you could listen to several times or is once enough? Explain.

STUDY QUESTIONS

1. Chamber ensembles are small groups that perform in _____ settings. (p. 263)
2. The favorite chamber ensemble format for composers since the late 1700s is (p. 263)
    A.   The string quintet
    B.   The small string orchestra
    C.   The string quartet
    D.   The woodwind quintet

3. The typical string quartet has (p. 263)

    A.   A violin, a viola, a cello, and a bass

    B.   2 violins, a viola, and a cello

    C.   A violin, a viola, a cello, and a piano

    D.·   A violin, a viola, and 2 cellos

4. The instruments of the quartet are capable of producing unique soloistic sounds and lush, blending sonorities. (p. 263)

    A.   True

    B.   False

5. One of the first composers to write for string quartets was (p. 263)

    A.   Beethoven

    B.   Mozart

    C.   Schubert

    D.   Haydn

6. The earliest quartets were derived from dance suites and called _____. (p. 263)

7. The Baroque trio sonata consisted of (p. 264)

    A.   Four players and four musical lines

    B.   Three players and four musical lines

    C.   Four players and three musical lines

    D.   Two players and three musical lines

8. The earliest quartets required a continuo part. (p. 264)

    A.   True

    B.   False

9. In early quartets, most composers favored the first violin part with the most difficult passages. (p. 264)

    A.   True

    B.   False

10. The other parts played a more accompanimental role in order to retain the _____ tradition of the divertimenti. (p. 264)

11. The quartet gradually developed into a unified texture built on sharing _____ _____. (p. 264)

12. Haydn first showed tendencies toward _____ _____ in his quartets. (p. 264)

13. The above named technique eventually became the basis of (p. 264)

    A.   Sonata-allegro form

    B.   Minuet and trio form

    C.   Theme and variations form

    D.   Rondo form

14. Haydn eventually expanded this writing technique into his

    A.   Quintets

    B.   Divertimenti

    C.   Symphonies

    D.   Oratorios

15. The technique of plucking the strings is referred to as (p. 264)

    A.   Martellato

    B.   Pizzicato

    C.   Col legno

    D.   Arco

16. The technique of bowing the strings is referred to as (p.264)

    A.   Martellato

    B.   Pizzicato

    C.   Col legno

    D.   Arco

17. The Classical string quartet reached its zenith with (p. 265)

    A.   Beethoven

    B.   Mozart

    C.   Schubert

    D.   Haydn

18. The last five quartets and fugue by Beethoven are considered to be some of the most intellectual compositions of his career. (p. 266)

    A.   True

    B.   False

19. The last quartets by Beethoven are _____, concise, and structurally unique. (p. 266)

20. Beethoven uses _____ technique in the first movement of his *Quartet in C-sharp Minor, Op. 131.* (p. 266)

21. In his last quartets, Beethoven demands _____ _____ from the players to produce rich, full sonorities. (p. 266)

22. Romantic composers such as Schubert and Brahms developed rich sonorities with increased levels of _____ and _____ _____. (p. 267)

23. A string articulation in which the pitch fluctuates slightly higher and lower is called (p. 267)

    A.   Marcato

    B.   Tremolo

    C.   Trill

    D.   Double-stopping

24. The string technique in which two notes are played simultaneously is called (p. 267)

    A.   Marcato

    B.   Tremolo

    C.   Trill

    D.   Double-stopping

25. The string quartets of Bartók demonstrate the durability of _____ and _____ form. (p. 267)

26. The melodies of Bartók's quartets are (p. 267)

    A.   Smooth and flowing

    B.   Smooth and mellow

    C.   Angular and powerful

    D.   Angular and mellow

27. Bartók's second quartet is stated to be in A minor and actually (p. 267)

    A.   Is centered around the pitch A

    B.   Is in A minor

    C.   Is in A major

    D.   Is centered around the pitch C

28. The second movement of Bartók's *String Quartet No. 2, Op. 17* is (p. 268)

    A.   In rondo form and very consonant

    B.   In sonata-allegro form and very dissonant

    C.   In scherzo and trio form and very consonant

    D.   In rondo form and very dissonant

29. With the works of Schoenberg, the string quartet slipped into the world of _____. (p. 268)

30. In Schoenberg's quartets, the local rhythm defied _____ _____ patterns and melodies became more _____. (p. 268)

31. Melodic ideas seem more _____ than tuneful. (p. 268)

32. Why do string quartets rarely find mass appeal? (p. 270)

    _____

33. Which of the following is NOT true of the Turtle Island String Quartet? (p. 270)

    A.   It is comprised of four composer/arrangers

    B.   The four members have well-developed improvisational skills

    C.   The four members double on guitar when necessary

    D.   The four members have solid traditional music backgrounds

34. The quartet *Street Stuff* is a hybrid of Classical styles with (p. 270)

   A.   Jazz and Bluegrass

   B.   Jazz and Gospel

   C.   Gospel and Country

   D.   Country and Folk

35. In this quartet, the cello is often relegated to playing a strict rhythmic bass line called _____.

   (p. 270)

36. The above named style of bass line is popular in swing. (p. 270)

   A.   True

   B.   False

37. Recent efforts in writing string quartets have been developed by using (p. 271)

   A.   Computers

   B.   Woodwinds rather than strings

   C.   Chainsaws

   D.   Strings with brass

38. Contemporary composers no longer find the quartet a vibrant medium for developing and expressing compositional thought. (p. 271)

   A.   True

   B.   False

TOPIC 7, SOUNDS FROM THE UNITED STATES

I. Introduction (pp. 272-273)

    A. Music in the United States cannot be characterized by a single style

    B. Use of folk music ideas in concert music makes the concert music unique

    C. American styles have been influenced by Western European and African music

    D. Before the 20th century, American composers were overshadowed by European composers

        1. Jazz, blues, and gospel emerged in the early decades of the 20th century

        2. American composers blended European practices with the new American popular styles

        3. Several American composers rose to prominence

            a. Aaron Copland

            b. Charles Ives

            c. George Gershwin

            d. Duke Ellington

        4. These composers illustrate the diversity of American music

    E. Nationalism has been a part of music history for several years

        1. Use of folk material is an essential characteristic

        2. The sound of a culture is also an important characteristic

II. CHARLES IVES (pp. 273-276; see biography, p. 274)

    A. One of the most innovative composers of the early 20th century

        1. Music is filled with early American themes

        2. Music is so different it cannot be classified by any school of composition

        3. Ives has become the definition of American uniqueness

    B. Ives wrote uniquely structured works

        1. *Second Piano Sonata* (the *Concord Sonata*)

            a. Each movement is a musical portrait titled after an American writer

                i. Emerson

                ii. Hawthorne

                iii. The Alcotts

                iv. Thoreau

            b. The work is built around the motive of Beethoven's *Symphony No. 5*

            c. Also wrote a series of essays to accompany the sonata--*Essays Before a Sonata*

                i. Commentaries on the authors for whom the movements are named

                ii. Do not discuss the music

        2. Composed five symphonies and other orchestral works

            a. All contain surprising and imaginative textures

    b.   Example: *Three Places in New England*

        i.   Portrays childhood memory of two marching bands playing different music

        ii. Reproduces the environmental effect of several effects occurring simultaneously

        iii. Creates excitingly real dissonance

C. Ives's music is free of convention

    1. Music changed quickly from extreme dissonance to sentimental consonance

    2. Music is diverse but hinged around a firm, emotional background in the church

        a.   Used hymn tunes in dramatic contrast to unstable dissonant textures

        b.   Example: *The Unanswered Question*, the final answer is a statement of an old hymn

    3. Patriotic themes were favorite sources in his music

    4. Other works, notably for organ or chorus, use two different tonal centers simultaneously--
POLYTONALITY

D. Though a very private person, Ives is remembered as a colorful individual

    1. Very talented businessman

        a.   Instrumental in establishing life insurance in the United States

        b.   Wrote an effective book about selling

    2. Worked on compositions that could never be completed

        a.   Example: *Universe Symphony*, meant to be performed by all humanity on every
hill and dale

    3. Writing style inspired experimental and nontraditional tendencies in later composers

    4. Ives takes a unique position in American history

        a.   Transcendentalist

        b.   Businessman

        c.   Writer

        d.   Composer

E. LISTING NOTES: *General William Booth Enters into Heaven* (pp. 275-276)

III. GEORGE GERSHWIN (pp. 276-277; see biography, p. 277)

A. The music of Gershwin crosses over three different music traditions

    1. Classical: music is sophisticated, intelligent, immediately appealing

    2. Commercial: genius song writer

    3. Jazz: many of his songs have become standards for improvisation

B. Gershwin's unique musical style is familiar to perhaps more Americans than any other composer

C. Example: *Rhapsody in Blue*

    1. Established Gershwin as a significant composer of concert music

    2. Commissioned by Paul Whiteman

    3. Originally written for jazz band, most commonly performed by orchestra and solo pianist

4. Piece incorporates jazz elements but is not jazz in the strictest sense

5. It does not conform to the standard solo concerto

6. Form does not follow traditional concerto structures

7. Jazz-flavored concert music with rich melodies and harmonies

8. LISTENING NOTES: *Rhapsody In Blue* (pp. 279-280)

   D. Example: *Porgy and Bess*

1. Combines Gershwin's distinctive style with folk-like sounds

2. Syncopations and blue notes intensify the melodic lines

3. Initially had trouble finding a place in American music

     a. Unique musical style

     b. Subject matter dealing with the lives and struggles of black Americans in Charleston, South Carolina

4. Characters are realistic with believable personalities

5. Characters deal with problems similar to those found in most earlier operas

IV. AARON COPLAND (pp. 277-283; see biography, pp. 281-282)

   A. Copland was a versatile composer by 1930

   B. His music was typical of 20th-century composers

1. Dissonant

2. Powerful

3. Concise

   C. During the Depression, Copland moved to a more accessible musical style for the average concert-goer

   D. Wrote in several musical genres

1. For schools

2. For radio

3. Film music

4. Chamber music

5. Opera

6. Symphonies

   E. Music is best remembered for its pictures of folklore

   F. The music from his ballets is commonly performed in concert without the accompanying dance

1. Most famous ballets appeared within a few years of each other

     a. *Billy the Kid*

     b. *Rodeo*

     c. *Appalachian Spring*

2. Contains syncopated, percussive rhythms

3. Very tonal and melodic

4. LISTENING NOTES: "Hoedown" from *Rodeo* (pp. 282-283)

V. EDWARD KENNEDY "DUKE" ELLINGTON (pp. 283-286; see biography, pp. 283-284)

    A. Jazz is an art form unique to the United States

        1. A history of performances rather than of detailed compositions

        2. Musical ideas were most often worked out in an improvisational environment

        3. A need for arrangers and composers grew with the development of dance bands

    B. Ellington was a unique composer, arranger, pianist, and band leader

        1. Relied on the improvisational skills of specific performers to add unique instrumental colors

            a. Johnny Hodges

            b. Cootie Williams

        2. Ellington built compositions around the sounds of specific individuals

    C. Ellington was a prolific composer

        1. Copyrighted 952 compositions

        2. Perhaps the first jazz composer to write in a wide spectrum of styles

            a. Sacred concerts

            b. Suites

            c. Musicals

            d. Film scores

            e. Ballet

        3. Music is loose and free and allows for long improvisations

        4. Some songs were compared to Debussy

            a. Similar chord constructions

            b. Rich chords harmonize nearly every note

            c. Harmonic vocabulary an important part of his musical identity

        5. LISTENING NOTES: *Sophisticated Lady* (p. 285)

EXERCISES

1. Listen to the second movement ("Putnam's Camp") of *Three Places in New England* by Charles Ives. What is the form of this movement? Describe the instrumentation. Is this played by a typical orchestra or are other instruments added? What is the texture like? Does it sound as if several things are going on at the same time? Can you identify the short quotations of patriotic songs that Ives uses in this piece? What is the harmony like? Are there sections of polytonality or is there just one basic tonal center throughout the piece? How does this compare with other nationalist pieces (such as Mussorgsky or Bartók) that you have heard?

2. Listen to *Prelude for Piano No. 1* by George Gershwin. What is the form of this prelude? What jazz elements are present in this work? What classical elements are present in this work? Is the harmony basically tonal or is it very dissonant? Does it have an improvisational quality to it or does the piece sound composed? What else can be said about this piece?

3. Listen to the seventh movement of *Appalachian Spring* ballet suite by Aaron Copland. This is a set of variations on a Shaker hymn called "Simple Gifts." Describe the different variations that Copland devises for this movement. How does he treat the melody? Is this similar to other sets of variations that have been studied in this book? Why or why not? How does Copland use the orchestra for color in this piece? How does he use solo instruments against the background of the orchestra? Does this piece seem tonal or is there a lot of dissonance present in the work?

4. Listen to *Concerto for Cootie* by Duke Ellington. What is the form of this piece? This piece features trumpeter Cootie Williams; describe the various sounds that Williams achieves of the trumpet. How does he get some of these sounds? What are the concerto elements of this piece? Describe the different tone colors that are presented by the rest of the band. How do these compare or contrast with Williams's trumpet? What musical elements (tone color, tempo, texture, etc.), are used by Ellington to define the form of this piece?

STUDY QUESTIONS

1. Music in the United States is characterized by a single style. (p. 272)
   A. True
   B. False

2. American music has been most strongly influenced by the music from which two continents? (p. 272)
   A. _____
   B. _____

3. With what folk styles was concert music blended to create a unique American art music? (p. 272)
   A. _____
   B. _____
   C. _____

4. Music that uses folk songs as the basis of a style is called (pp. 272-273)
   A. Exotic
   B. Neoclassical
   C. Nationalist
   D. Sociopolitical

5. The composer who has become identified with America's uniqueness is (p. 273)

   A.   Charles Ives

   B.   George Gershwin

   C.   Aaron Copland

   D.   Duke Ellington

6. The music of the above named composer cannot be categorized into a specific school of composition. (p. 273)

   A.   True

   B.   False

7. In this composer's *Second Piano Sonata*, the movements are named for (p. 273)

   A.   National parks and landmarks

   B.   American writers from New England

   C.   Important Civil War battles

   D.   Important Revolutionary War battles

8. What environmental effect is reproduced in this composer's *Three Places in New England*? (p. 273)

   _____

9. This effect was inspired by hearing two bands playing different songs at the same time. (p. 273)

   A.   True

   B.   False

10. Much of the music by this composer centers around a firm, emotional background in (p. 273)

    A.   The church

    B.   Philosophy

    C.   Politics

    D.   Rhetoric

11. What musical types are used in this composer's works as points of security against unstable dissonant textures? (p. 273)

    A.   Patriotic songs

    B.   Folk songs

    C.   Popular songs

    D.   Hymns

12. The use of one or more key centers at the same time is called _____. (p. 273)

13. Although a talented composer, Ives earned his living in what field? (p. 273)

    A.   Retail business

    B.   Life insurance

    C.   Real estate

    D.   Broadway producer

14. For what reason is Ives's *Universe Symphony* impossible to perform? (p. 276)

_____

15. What three musical traditions influenced Gershwin's music? (p. 276)

   A. _____

   B. _____

   C. _____

16. The work that established Gershwin as a composer of concert music was _____ ___

   _____. (p. 276)

17. The above named work was originally written for (p. 276)

   A.   Piano and orchestra

   B.   The New York Metropolitan Opera

   C.   Paul Whiteman's jazz/dance band

   D.   The film *The Jazz Singer*

18. This piece is considered jazz because it uses many jazz elements of the day. (p. 276)

   A.   True

   B.   False

19. This piece does not conform to the expectations of traditional solo concertos. (p. 276)

   A.   True

   B.   False

20. Gershwin combined his unique style with folklike sounds to create what opera? (p. 276)

   A.   *Of Thee I Sing*

   B.   *The Girl of the Golden West*

   C.   *Appalachian Spring*

   D.   *Porgy and Bess*

21. The soaring melodies of this work are intensified by the use of _____ and

   blue notes. (p. 276)

22. What two reasons are given for the difficulty that this opera had in finding a place in American

   music? (p. 276)

   A. _____

   B. _____

23. The characters in this opera deal with problems similar to those in most early romantic operas. (p. 276)

   A.   True

   B.   False

24. The three musical traits associated with Copland and other 20th-century composers are (p. 277)

    A. _____

    B. _____

    C. _____

25. During the Depression, Copland's music became stylistically more accessible to (p. 277)

    A. European avant gardists

    B. The average concert-goer

    C. Wealthy art patrons

    D. Broadway show producers

26. Copland's music is best remembered for its pictures of _____. (p. 279)

27. Name two of Copland's popular ballets from 1938-1944 (p. 279)

    A. _____

    B. _____

28. The music from these ballets are most commonly performed to accompany the dancing. (p. 279)

    A. True

    B. False

29. The music has _____ and _____ rhythms. (p. 279)

30. Copland's music is typically (p. 279)

    A. Tonal and melodic

    B. Strongly dissonant and non-melodic

    C. Atonal with angular melodies

    D. Dissonant with distorted melodies

31. The technique in which a performer slides up or down in pitch without distinct pitches being heard is called _____. (p. 279)

32. A musical art form that is unique to the United States is _____. (p. 284)

33. Jazz is a history of detailed compositions. (p. 284)

    A. True

    B. False

34. In jazz, most musical ideas are worked out in _____ environment. (p. 284)

35. Arrangers and composers were needed for the big bands in order to (p. 284)

    A. Create million-selling records

    B. Run the business end of the big band

    C. Organize the musical activities of many musicians

    D. Hire exceptional talents for which to compose

36. Ellington was well known for his abilities as a _____, _____, and _____. (p. 284)

37. Ellington's compositions relied on the improvisational skills of Johnny Hodges and Cootie Williams to add (p. 284)

   A.   Unique instrumental colors

   B.   Chaos to stability

   C.   Sentimental expression

   D.   Stability to confusion

38. Ellington typically built his compositions around the sound of the instruments alone rather than the sound of individual performers. (p. 284)

   A.   True

   B.   False

39. Ellington composed a ballet. (p. 284)

   A.   True

   B.   False

40. Ellington's music has been characterized as being (p. 284)

   A.   Strict and confined

   B.   Loose and free

   C.   Strict and atonal

   D.   Loose and polytonal

41. Ellington's compositions do not allow room for long improvisations. (p. 284)

   A.   True

   B.   False

42. Ellington's _____ vocabulary was an important part of his style. (p. 284)

43. Because of similar chord constructions, some of Ellington's works have been compared with (p. 284)

   A.   Schoenberg

   B.   Dvorák

   C.   Stravinsky

   D.   Debussy

44. Name three places where composers are found in America according to Megill. (p. 286)

   A.   _____

   B.   _____

   C.   _____

TOPIC 8, ETHNOMUSICOLOGY

I. Introduction (pp. 287-288)

    A. There is no single example of music that represents North American culture

        1. There are many cultural and ethnic backgrounds in America

        2. The diversity in our culture is responsible for its richness and complexity

    B. There is a wide spectrum of musical styles around the world

        1. There remains a sense of global unity in the arts

        2. By examining other cultures we see our own culture in a new light

        3. If we can learn to value the many styles in our culture, we can learn to value other cultures

    C. The music studied so far in this text spans over 1000 years

        1. Not all sounds have been familiar or likable

        2. Through study these sounds have become more understandable

        3. This music has had a direct impact on our culture

    D. ETHNOMUSICOLOGY

        1. The study of music of specific ethnic groups

        2. Music is studied in light of tradition and culture

        3. Ethnomusicologists study the details of music specific to different cultures

            a. Can trace a culture's heritage and development

            b. Often deal with subgroupings within a culture that may seem homogeneous to outsiders

II. Music from Other Cultures (p. 288)

    A. Music from non-Western cultures have the same components as Western European music

        1. Rhythm

        2. Melody

        3. Form

    B. The priorities of these musical components may differ in other cultures

        1. Melody may be most important in one culture

        2. Rhythm may be more important in another culture

    C. Familiarity and exposure make the music understandable and enjoyable

        1. Music from other cultures may sound fascinating or strange at first listen

        2. New listeners may lack an association with that culture's traditions

        3. Musical elements that sound similar to the music of one's own culture will naturally make more sense

    B. Film soundtracks give an idea of some of the sounds unique to other cultures

        1. Film soundtracks are not necessarily accurate representations of another culture's music

2. Often uses familiar instruments and scales with melodic and harmonic alterations to give the impression of another country

III. Folk Music: Unique Sounds from Unique Cultures (pp. 288-289)

    A. The world of sound has become more integrated over the last twenty years

        1. Growth in audio and video communications

        2. Documentaries and satellite communications bring the arts from other countries directly into the home

    B. Every country has a unique musical development that originated with its folk music

    C. The older an ethnic culture, the more significant the roots of its folk music

    D. American music has mostly developed alongside technology

        1. American music has been recorded and transported all over the world

        2. American music is to some extent the world's music

    E. In many countries, folk music is a vital part of heritage and ethnic identity

    F. Folk music and ORAL TRADITION

        1. Information, history, and culture were communicated orally from generation to generation

        2. Folk music is shaped, changed, and communicated mostly through oral tradition

        3. Composers or originators of most folk music are mostly unknown

        4. Uses of music in society include

            a. To communicate history, society rules, and morals

            b. In some societies, music plays a part in religion and philosophy

            c. Music is therefore tied to a culture's needs and beliefs

    G. The organic material that develops into any culture's art music is found in its folk music

IV. Dividing the Octave into Scales (p. 289)

    A. The influence of folk music on the development of art music is important

    B. The level of influence varies from country to country

    C. Music of other cultures sounds different primarily because of the use of different scale systems

    D. The octave is divided differently in many cultures

        1. CHROMATIC SCALE

            a. Divides the octave into twelve equal half steps

            b. The basis of Western European music

        2. PENTATONIC SCALE

            a. Divides the octave into five different pitches

            b. The fundamental scale in much Oriental music

        3. TRITONIC SCALE

            a. A three-note scale

            b. Used in African music

4. HEPTATONIC SCALE

    a. A seven-note scale

    b. Also used in African music

    c. The tritonic and heptatonic systems are often combined with melodic patterns built from whole steps and half steps

5. MICROTONAL SCALE

    a. Include intervals smaller than a half step

    b. Used in the music of India

    c. Very complex scale patterns

V. Rhythm (p. 291)

  A. Rhythm varies dramatically from culture to culture

  B. POLYRHYTHMS

    1. The simultaneous use of two or more contrasting rhythms

    2. These rhythms often conflict with and obscure the beat

    3. Each rhythm is usually very complex in itself

    4. Often used in the music of Africa, India, and Latin America

    5. Rhythmic patterns in American music are simple in comparison

      a. American music is based on melodic and harmonic functions

      b. Melody and harmony is supported by regular, repeated rhythmic patterns

  C. MODULATED RHYTHM

    1. A constant movement from one meter to another in a short period of time

    2. No regular pattern of beats

    3. Found in music of the 20th century

    4. Sometimes referred to as "shifting meter"

VI. Harmony (p. 291)

  A. Primarily a development in Western European music

  B. The DRONE

    1. The most basic of harmonic concepts

    2. A long, sustained sound used to support a freely floating melody

    3. Consists of one or two pitches

    4. A very early form of harmonic development

    5. Example: Bagpipe music of Scotland

  C. The early stages of polyphony developed as multiple melodies slowly became harmony

  D. HETEROPHONY

    1. A sophisticated form of harmony found in some folk music

    2. A melody is sung in unison by two performers, but is varied or ornamented by each

3. Produces a unique combination of melodic ideas

4. An improvised form of harmony

VII. Sounds from Several Cultures (pp. 290-296)

    A. Japan, Imperial Sho Koto Chant: *Gagaku* (p. 290)

        1. Performed by male singers chanting a slow, low traditional dance

        2. Accompaniment

            a. Koto

                i. Plucked string instrument

                ii. Primary source of percussive rhythm

            b. Sho

                i. A small mouth organ with small pipes

                ii. Plays unison melody four octaves higher than the singers

                iii. Sho player deliberately goes slightly in and out of tune against the singers, creating feeling of tension and release

    B. India, Sanai Gath: *Raga Kaphi* (pp. 291-292)

        1. Sitar

            a. Fretted Indian string instrument

            b. Frets are movable, allow for microtonal scales

            c. Probably the Indian instrument that is most familiar to Americans

        2. Drums: Tabla and Baya

            a. Accompany the sitar rhythmically

            b. Play sophisticated rhythmic cycles called TALAS

                i. Rhythmic cycle is repeated several times by the drums

                ii. Varies in complexity from two or three notes to very long patterns

                iii. Raga is improvised over the tala

        3. Sanai

            a. Double reed melodic instrument

            b. Note sliding (GLISSANDO) between pitches

        4. The melody is derived from a traditional melodic pattern called a RAGA

            a. There are hundreds of different ragas on which to base a performance

            b. The octave in Indian music is divided into twenty-two notes

            c. A raga is a scale of pitches selected from this microtonal series

            d. The selected raga and tala are used to build complex improvisations

    C. Bali, Indonesia, Gamelan Orchestra: *Gender Wajang* (p. 293)

        1. Consists of several types and sizes of tuned percussion instruments

        2. Instruments are tuned to a pentatonic scale

3. Dynamic levels shift throughout the composition

4. Texture contains many syncopated ideas within a fluid tempo

5. Accompaniment uses freely improvised ornaments and rhythms

6. Performance ends with an increase in tempo and melodic activity

7. This style of music influenced Debussy who liked the rich, blended sound

D. China, Hu-kin and Butterfly harp (p. 294)

1. Hu-kin is a two-stringed bowed instrument

2. Butterfly harp has several short strings that are played by small bamboo hammers

3. Both instruments play the melody in unison

    a. Melody is based on a pentatonic scale

    b. Complex melodic shape is due partly to microtonal ornamentation

    c. Long phrases are contrasted with short phrases

    d. Phrasing pattern contrasts with the regular phrasing of Western music

E. Zululand, South Africa, Flutes and Body Harp (p. 295)

1. Performance

    a. Based on two simple, repetitive melodic ideas of three notes each

    b. Chant-like repetitions have very subtle variations in inflection

    c. Performance could probably continue for a long period of time

2. Flute has a very breathy sound

3. Body harp

    a. Bow harp with three strings

    b. Strings are strummed by the fingernails

    c. Tone is produced by a gourd resonator connected to the bow

F. Native American, Navajo: *Ribbon Dance* (p. 296)

1. Accompaniment

    a. Drum: stretched animal skin over a wooden resonator

    b. Shaker or rattle: beads strung around a gourd

    c. Typical of the sounds used to accompany Native American chant melodies

2. Performance

    a. Vocal quality is nasal

    b. Voice projects easily over the percussion accompaniment

    c. Melody is shared by the leader and two other singers

    d. CALL AND RESPONSE performance

        i. A musical dialogue between two musical sources

        ii. Leader states phrase

        iii. Other two singers join in on the repeated phrases

EXERCISES

1. Listen to as many other musical examples from other cultures as you can. You have five examples with which to compare other recordings. Listen to other examples from the six cultures discussed in the textbook. Branch out to listening to the music of other cultures from around the world. The main point is to become familiar with the music from other cultures. The more you can understand another culture's music, the more you can understand another culture.

2. In addition to listening to recorded examples of music, keep on the alert in your community for celebrations held by various cultural groups that will often include music as a part of the festivities. On many college campuses there are various ethnic student groups that have at least a yearly celebration of some kind that are open to the campus community and even the city community. There are interesting people to meet at these types of events and you can learn about other cultures' arts and music, traditional clothing, and, perhaps best of all, their cuisine.

STUDY QUESTIONS

1. What is responsible for the richness and complexity of American culture? (p. 287)
    A. Homogeneity
    B. Similarity
    C. Diversity
    D. Unity
2. Although there is a wide variety of musical styles around the world, there remains a sense of
    _____ _____ in the arts. (p. 287)
3. Although all music may not be familiar or likable, through study it becomes (p. 287)
    A. Understandable
    B. Confusing
    C. Boring
    D. Expendable
4. The study of musical styles of different ethnic groups is called _____. (p. 287)
5. In this discipline, music is studied in light of an ethnic group's _____ and
    _____. (p. 287)

6. Music can be used to trace an ethnic group's (p. 288)

    A.   Folklore and religion

    B.   Heritage and development

    C.   Language and morals

    D.   Language and customs

7. Musical components such as rhythm, melody, and form may have different priorities in different music. (p. 288)

    A.   True

    B.   False

8. Two elements that make music more understandable and enjoyable are (p. 288)

    A.   _____

    B.   _____

9. Music from other cultures may sound strange at first because the listener lacks a meaningful association with that culture's _____. (p. 288)

10. Musical elements that sound similar to one's own music usually will make more sense than the elements that are completely foreign. (p. 288)

    A.   True

    B.   False

11. One can gain an idea of another culture's music through _____ _____. (p. 288)

12. Music used in soundtracks to portray the music of another culture are usually accurate representations of that culture's music. (p. 288)

    A.   True

    B.   False

13. The world of music has become more integrated over the last twenty years because of the growth of _____ and _____ communications. (p. 288)

14. Every culture has a unique musical development that is generated by (p. 288)

    A.   Religious institutions

    B.   Folk music

    C.   Traditional ritual dances

    D.   Language and customs

15. Except for the music of native Americans, most American music has developed alongside (p. 288)

    A.   Big business

    B.   American sports

    C.   Hollywood productions

    D.   Electronic technology

16. In many countries, folk music is a vital part of _____ and _____

    _____. (p. 289)

17. Most folk music is shaped, altered, and communicated through (p. 289)

    A.   Intricate notation

    B.   Books of songs

    C.   Oral tradition

    D.   National Public Radio

18. In many case, the composer or originator of folk music is unknown. (p. 289)

    A.   True

    B.   False

19. In preliterate societies, songs may be used to relate _____, _____ _____,

    and _____. (p. 289)

20. In highly developed societies, music plays an important role in (p. 289)

    A.   Religion and philosophy

    B.   Religion and theater

    C.   Theater and commercialism

    D.   Philosophy and sports

21. Music is tied directly to a culture's needs and beliefs. (p. 289)

    A.   True

    B.   False

22. The organic material that develops into the art music associated with any culture comes from (p. 289)

    A.   Religious background

    B.   Major composers and performers

    C.   Dramatic heritage

    D.   Folk music

23. The level of influence that folk music exerts on art music varies from country to country. (p. 289)

    A.   True

    B.   False

24. One of the main differences between music of different cultures is heard in the division of (p. 289)

    A.   The fundamental note

    B.   The octave

    C.   The interval

    D.   The third

25. The scale which is constructed of twelve equal half steps is called (p. 289)

    A.   Pentatonic

    B.   Chromatic

    C.   Tritonic

    D.   Heptatonic

26. The scale named in question 25 is the basis of the music from (p. 289)

    A.   Africa

    B.   Eastern Asia

    C.   Western Europe

    D.   India

27. The scale in which the octave is divided into seven different pitches is called (p. 289)

    A.   Pentatonic

    B.   Chromatic

    C.   Tritonic

    D.   Heptatonic

28. The scale in which the octave is divided into five different pitches is called (p. 289)

    A.   Pentatonic

    B.   Chromatic

    C.   Tritonic

    D.   Heptatonic

29. The three note scale that is used in Africa and combined with melodies that use whole steps and half steps is called _____. (p. 289)

30. Scales in which the octave is divided into intervals that are less than a half step apart are called _____. (p. 289)

31. These complex scale patterns are found in the music of (p. 289)

    A.   Africa

    B.   Eastern Asia

    C.   Western Europe

    D.   India

32. A small, Japanese string instrument that is like a harp is (p. 290)

    A.   The hu-kin

    B.   The koto

    C.   The sitar

    D.   The sho

33. The Japanese instrument that is a small mouth organ is (p. 290)

    A.   The hu-kin

    B.   The koto

    C.   The sitar

    D.   The sho

34. Two or more complex, contrasting rhythms that are played against one another are called

    _____. (p. 291)

35. This rhythmic technique is frequently found in the music of _____, _____,

    and _____ _____. (p. 291)

36. The technique in which the meter shifts in a short period of time is called _____

    rhythm. (p. 291)

37. The above named technique results in a regular pattern of beats. (p. 291)

    A.   True

    B.   False

38. Harmony is primarily a Western concept. (p. 291)

    A.   True

    B.   False

39. One or two sustained pitches that support a free melody is called a _____. (p. 291)

40 The musical texture in which two instruments play the same melody in unison and each performer

    improvises ornaments simultaneously is called (p. 291)

    A.   Monophony

    B.   Homophony

    C.   Heterophony

    D.   Polyphony

41. The Indian instrument that is probably most familiar to American audiences is (p. 291)

    A.   The hu-kin

    B.   The koto

    C.   The sitar

    D.   The sho

42. On the above named instrument, the frets are movable in order to play _____

    scales. (p. 291)

43. The two drums that are used in traditional Indian music are called the _____ and the

    _____. (p. 291)

44. The complex rhythmic patterns played by these drums are called (p. 292)

   A.   Sanai

   B.   Talas

   C.   Polyrhythms

   D.   Ragas

45. The double reed instrument used in Indian music is called (p. 292)

   A.   Sanai

   B.   Talas

   C.   Polyrhythms

   D.   Ragas

46. The melody of Indian music is improvised from scale patterns called (p. 292)

   A.   Sanai

   B.   Talas

   C.   Polyrhythms

   D.   Ragas

47. The gamelan orchestra uses different types and sizes of untuned percussion instruments. (p. 293)

   A.   True

   B.   False

48. The gamelan orchestra makes use of the _____ scale. (p. 293)

49. The European composer who was influenced by the rich sonorities of the gamelan was (p. 293)

   A.   Schoenberg

   B.   Debussy

   C.   Stravinsky

   D.   Copland

50. The texture of gamelan music is characterized by syncopated ideas against a fluid tempo. (p. 293)

   A.   True

   B.   False

51. The two-stringed, bowed Chinese instrument discussed in this chapter is called (p. 294)

   A.   The hu-kin

   B.   The koto

   C.   The sitar

   D.   The sho

52. The Butterfly harp is played by (p. 294)

    A.   Drawing a bow across the strings

    B.   Plucking the strings with the fingernails

    C.   Striking the strings with small bamboo hammers

    D.   Plucking the strings with a bird's quill

53. The example of Chinese music is based on the _____ scale. (p. 294)

54. The South African body harp is played by (p. 295)

    A.   Drawing a bow across the strings

    B.   Plucking the strings with the fingernails

    C.   Striking the strings with small bamboo hammers

    D.   Plucking the strings with a bird's quill

55. The sound of the flute in the South African example is _____ compared to the focused
    flute sound of Europe and America. (p. 295)

56. The South African performance is based on two repetitive melodic ideas of _____
    notes. (p. 295)

57. The melody of this example is derived from (p. 289)

    A.   Pentatonic

    B.   Chromatic

    C.   Tritonic

    D.   Heptatonic

58. The Navajo musical example is accompanied by tuned percussion instruments. (p. 296)

    A.   True

    B.   False

59. The vocal quality of this example is _____ to project over the accompaniment. (p. 296)

60. This example uses a performance technique called (p. 296)

    A.   Polytonality

    B.   Sound poetry

    C.   Blues inflection

    D.   Call and response

TOPIC 9, COMPOSING FOR MUSICAL THEATER

I. Introduction (pp. 297-298)

    A. Musical theater has become a popular part of American and European society

    B. Musicals have grown in scope and flair since their beginnings in the late 1800s

    C. Many musicals use the technological advances associated with the stage and film

    D. The plot is communicated through song, empowered by music

    E. Balance between words and music shifted at each stage of development

        1. Understanding the words has always been the most important concern in musicals

        2. Orchestra size changed depending on the quality of the voices

        3. Increased use of amplification has allowed the orchestra to grow in size and volume

        4. Musical textures of modern musicals can be very dense and loud

    F. Musical theater today has become a multimedia spectacle.

        1. Visual aspects have developed along with the musical aspects

        2. All aspects of the performing arts are a part of musical theater

    G. Many musicals have been made into movies

        1. Movies differ dramatically from live performances

        2. Live performances are immediate and cannot be redone if mistakes happen

        3. Composers must anticipate the conditions for which music is written

        4. Stage productions and film productions of the same work vary considerably to conform to the performance medium

II. The Development of Musical Theater (pp. 298-308)

    A. A musical called *Black Crook* developed into a new form of musical entertainment

        1. First played in 1866

        2. Perhaps the first musical to have a continuous plot to unify a string of acts

    B. Musical theater had previously been referred to as MINSTREL SHOWS, BURLESQUE, or VAUDEVILLE

        1. Minstrel Show

            a. Early American touring groups

            b. Performed music and comedy

         2. Burlesque

            a. Early American form of entertainment

            b. Consists of skits, gags, and music

         3. Vaudeville

            a. Similar to minstrel shows

            b. Popular American entertainment in the early 20th century

4. All these types of shows had no story lines

5. Nothing more than a series of unrelated musical events

C. A mixture of European opera, operetta, and ballet merged into the American musical

   1. Earliest musical of this nature is considered to be *The Book* (1879)

   2. Songs and dances were woven into the plot

   3. The plot was concerned with present day events

   4. MUSICAL COMEDY became synonymous with musical theater

   5. Later plots would be more dramatic than comic

D. Musical composers in the early part of the 20th century

   1. George M. Cohan

     a. The first notable composer who helped to define the new style of musical theater

     b. His musical *Forty-Five Minutes from Broadway* (1906) was important in breaking ties with European tradition

   2. Jerome Kern

     a. Further developed the American style in New York during World War I

     b. Teamed with lyricist Oscar Hammerstein II to produce the first mature American musical, *Show Boat* (1927)

   3. George and Ira Gershwin

     a. Followed *Show Boat* with a political satire, *Of Thee I Sing* (1931)

     b. This musical won the Pulitzer Prize for drama

   4. Other leading composers were Irving Berlin and Cole Porter

   5. Richard Rodgers and Lorenz Hart were considered the most famous team of the 1930s

   6. The range of topics for plots during this period expanded greatly

   7. Themes moved from romantic love to controversial, even political, subjects

E. Perhaps the most successful team in the mid-20th century was Rodgers and Hammerstein

   1. *Oklahoma!* (1943)

     a. Provided the next major step in musical comedy

     b. Showed a new level of unity in music and lyrics, plot, and dance

     c. The drama successfully integrated song with plot

   2. Other commonly performed musicals by Rodgers and Hammerstein include

     a. *Carousel* (1945)

     b. *South Pacific* (1949)

     c. *The King and I* (1951)

     d. *The Sound of Music* (1959)

F. Musical theater is often considered to be the place where the impossible becomes possible

G. Individuals are characterized by the music they sing

H. Transitions from spoken dialogue to singing is difficult to manage

    1. Opera solved the problem by using RECITATIVE in place of spoken dialogue

    2. Early movie musicals solved the problem with plots concerning singers or dancers

        a. Relatively natural for characters to begin singing or dancing

        b. Often relates a show within a show (and rehearsals for that show)

    3. *Oklahoma!*

        a. Was instrumental in moving away from shows about singers and dancers

        b. Singing and dancing became expressive of the mood and condition of the actors and their roles

I. LEONARD BERNSTEIN (see biography, pp. 301-302) and *West Side Story*

    1. *West Side Story* is a mixture of plot and conditions

    2. The plot is about gang culture

    3. The music holds the drama together

        a. The musical is shaped by developing themes and motives

        b. The last scene is a resolution of the musical tension built up in the last several scenes

        c. The drama is effective because it is woven together by themes and motives

    4. The BOOK (lyrics or libretto) is by Stephen Sondheim, based on *Romeo and Juliet*

    5. The music is based on jazz styles of the 1940s and 1950s

        a. Rhythm swings

        b. Dancing is based on jazz movement

    6. LISTENING NOTES: "Cool" from *West Side Story* (pp. 302-303)

J. Musical theater since the 1920s has been a reflection of the times

    1. This is most evident in the musicals of the 1960s and 1970s

    2. *Fiddler on the Roof* (1964)

        a. Follows the plight of oppressed Russian Jews during the Russian Revolution

        b. Story focused on aspects of ethnic diversity

    3. *Hair* (1967) and *Grease* (1972)

        a. *Hair* is a political/social production

        b. *Grease* is a 1950s rock 'n' roll musical

        c. Both are time pieces of American popular art

        d. The statements are dated today, but relevant in their time

    4. *A Chorus Line*

        a. The longest running show in history

        b. Shows the plight of dancers in a competitive world

        c. Characters try to survive in a very competitive environment

        d. The plot returns to a show within a show

5. *The Three-Penny Opera* (1928)

    a. Consists of more controversial topics

    b. Based on the 18th century ballad opera *The Beggar's Opera* (1728)

    c. Plot deals with a subculture of beggars and thieves

    d. Portrays a cynical outlook on society

    e. Has been successful in Europe and America

K. ANDREW LLOYD WEBBER (see biography, pp. 306-307)

    1. The popularity of musical theater has suffered over the last few years except for the works of Andrew Lloyd Webber

    2. Andrew Lloyd Webber's musicals have kept playing for years simultaneously in London, New York, and Los Angeles

    3. Andrew Lloyd Webber's productions

        a. Are expensive, flashy, and spectacular

        b. Have strange, unbelievable plots and settings

        c. Are well received because of their newness

    4. *The Phantom of the Opera* (1987)

        a. Enjoys a unique association with both opera and musical theater

            i. Subject matter requires the use of operatic voices

            ii. Also requires a large orchestra

            iii. Musically ambitious compared to traditional examples of musical theater

        b. The work has appealed to fans of both opera and popular music

        c. Comparisons with opera are unquestionable

            i. There is a new balance between sung and spoken dialogue

            ii. Spoken dialogue is reduced to a minimum

            iii. The music never stops, the orchestra is always actively contributing to the emotional development of the plot

            iv. Recitative is used successfully in musical theater for the first time

            v. Lines of text are set without rhyme or regular phrasing

            vi. The text drives the flow of the music

            vii. Uses the ENSEMBLE FINALE

                1. Four or five individuals sing separate and overlapping lines

                2. Each part expresses a different emotion with a different text

                3. Patterned after the ensemble finales of 19th-century opera

        d. There are also elements taken from rock musicals such as *Hair* or *Tommy*

        e. LISTING NOTES: *The Phantom of the Opera*, Act I, Scenes 4 and 5 (pp. 307-308)

EXERCISES

As in observing and evaluating conductors, the best way to evaluate a musical is to attend a live performance of a show. In almost every community there are high school groups, university groups, and amateur community theater groups and one of these groups will produce a musical such as those discussed in this topic chapter. Some performances occur maybe once a year, or perhaps even every other year, but there are musicals performed in most communities. Be on the lookout also for performances in or near your community of traveling productions of musicals, usually advertised as "road productions" or "off-Broadway" shows. These are usually very good, very exciting performances. Be observant of the audience of which you are a part in these performances. How others react to the dialogue and musical and dance numbers is sometimes as interesting as the performance itself. Go and enjoy a live performance of a musical at least once.

STUDY QUESTIONS

1. Musical theater has become a popular part of American and European society. (p. 297)

    A.   True

    B.   False

2. Musicals have grown in scope using many of the technological advances associated with stage and _____. (p. 297)

3. At the heart of contemporary musicals is a plot that is communicated through (p. 297)

    A.   Dialogue

    B.   Song

    C.   Dance

    D.   Recitative

4. The balance between words and music shifted at different stages of the musical's development. (p. 297)

    A.   True

    B.   False

5. The quality of the music has always been the most important concern in musicals. (p. 297)

    A.   True

    B.   False

6. Musical theater today is a _____ spectacle involving all branches of the performing arts. (p. 297)

7. Which of the following is NOT true of the difference between stage and film productions? (p. 298)

    A. Film can be edited into a "perfect" performance

    B. Film requires much more music

    C. Film is immediate and cannot be redone

    D. Film usually requires a much larger orchestra

8. Stage productions and film productions of the same musical need not vary in performance. (p. 298)

    A. True

    B. False

9. Name the three types of 19th-century American entertainment that led to the development of the musical. (p. 298)

    A. _____

    B. _____

    C. _____

10. These shows had no story line and were a series of unrelated _____ _____.
    (p. 298)

11. The term that became synonymous with musical theater in the late 1800s was _____
    _____. (p. 299)

12. The first notable composer to help define a new form of musical theater was (p. 299)

    A. George Gershwin

    B. Jerome Kern

    C. Richard Rodgers

    D. George M. Cohan

13. The composer who is credited with developing an American style of musical theater during World War I was (p. 299)

    A. George Gershwin

    B. Jerome Kern

    C. Richard Rodgers

    D. George M. Cohan

14. The first mature American musical was *Show Boat* by _____ and his lyricist _____
    _____. (p. 299)

15. The composer who received the Pulitzer Prize for the musical *Of Thee I Sing* was (p. 299)

    A. George Gershwin

    B. Jerome Kern

    C. Richard Rodgers

    D. George M. Cohan

16. The lyricist for *Of Thee I Sing* was (p. 299)

    A.   Oscar Hammerstein II

    B.   Lorenz Hart

    C.   Ira Gershwin

    D.   Stephen Sondheim

17. The two composers who, with Gershwin and Kern, were the leading composers of musicals in the 1930s were (p. 299)

    A.   _____

    B.   _____

18. The most famous team of the 1930s was composer Richard Rodgers and lyricist (p. 299)

    A.   Oscar Hammerstein II

    B.   Lorenz Hart

    C.   Ira Gershwin

    D.   Bertolt Brecht

19. Topics for plots expanded from themes of romantic love to plots that were _____ and _____. (p. 299)

20. The Rodgers and Hammerstein musical that showed a new level of unity between music, dancing, and story line was (p. 299)

    A.   *South Pacific*

    B.   *Show Boat*

    C.   *Oklahoma!*

    D.   *The Sound of Music*

21. How did early film musicals make the transition from dialogue to musical numbers easier? (p. 299)

    _____

22. The Bernstein musical about gang culture is (p. 300)

    A.   *Candide*

    B.   *Wonderful Town*

    C.   *On the Town*

    D.   *West Side Story*

23. The above named musical is held together by the music which develops _____ and _____. (p. 301)

24. Since the above statement is true, Bernstein approaches the musical like (p. 301)

    A.   A symphonic composer

    B.   A dramatic composer

    C.   A comedic composer

    D.   An operatic composer

25. What is required to draw the listener into the plot of a musical? (p. 301)

_____

26. The book or libretto for *West Side Story* was written by lyricist (p. 302)

    A.   Oscar Hammerstein II

    B.   Lorenz Hart

    C.   Ira Gershwin

    D.   Stephen Sondheim

27. The plot of *West Side Story* is loosely based on (p. 302)

    A.   *Cyrano de Bergerac*

    B.   *Romeo and Juliet*

    C.   *The Taming of the Shrew*

    D.   *Beat It*

28. Since the 1920s, musical theater has been a reflection of the times. (p. 303)

    A.   True

    B.   False

29. The post-1960 musical that focused on aspects of ethnic diversity is (p. 303)

    A.   *Hair*

    B.   *A Chorus Line*

    C.   *Fiddler on the Roof*

    D.   *Man of La Mancha*

30. The musical that was a political statement in the late 1960s is (p. 303)

    A.   *Hair*

    B.   *A Chorus Line*

    C.   *Fiddler on the Roof*

    D.   *Man of La Mancha*

31. The musical that shows performers in a very competitive environment is (p. 303)

    A.   *Hair*

    B.   *A Chorus Line*

    C.   *Fiddler on the Roof*

    D.   *Man of La Mancha*

32. The musical *The Three-Penny Opera* was written by the team of (p. 304)

    A.   Rodgers and Hammerstein

    B.   George and Ira Gershwin

    C.   Rodgers and Hart

    D.   Weill and Brecht

33. *The Three-Penny Opera* was based on an old English _____ _____. (p. 304)

34. *The Three-Penny Opera* paints a very rosy picture of the subculture of beggars and thieves. (p. 304)

    A.   True

    B.   False

35. The popularity of musical theater has declined in the last few years except for the successes of

    _____. (p. 304)

36. Which of the following is NOT true of singers of musical theater? (p. 304)

    A.   They have a more natural-sounding voice that is easily understood

    B.   They have an expansive, wide range of notes

    C.   Compared with opera voices, their range and flexibility is limited

    D.   They have a clear voice to draw the listener into the plot

37. *The Phantom of the Opera* is often compared with opera because the subject deals with opera

    and the work requires operatic voices and a large orchestra. (p. 304)

    A.   True

    B.   False

38. In *The Phantom of the Opera*, spoken dialogue is reduced to a minimum resulting in (p. 304)

    _____

39. The orchestra actively contributes to the _____ _____ of

    the plot. (p. 304)

40. What operatic element is used successfully for the first time in musical theater in *The Phantom of the*

    Opera ? (p. 304)

    A.   Coloratura singing

    B.   Da capo aria

    C.   Recitative

    D.   Bel canto singing

41. Because the text drives the flow of the music, *The Phantom of the Opera* is more like commercial

    music than opera. (p. 305)

    A.   True

    B.   False

42. Another comparison to opera is found in the _____ _____ of *The Phantom*

    of the Opera. (p. 305)

43. List two characteristics of the ensemble finale. (p. 305)

    A.   _____

    B.   _____

44. Andrew Lloyd Webber's association with classical music is paralleled by an equal association with

    _____. (p. 305)

TOPIC 10, COMPOSING IN THE STUDIO

I. Introduction (pp. 309-310)

    A. The recording studio is a common environment for composers and performers of most contemporary styles

        1. Performers play to microphones as well as to live audiences

        2. There is a great deal of pressure in the recording studio for the "perfect' performance

        3. The recording studio gives performers the opportunity to fix mistakes

        4. However, it is expensive and time consuming to rerecord

    B. Studio musicians play in an isolated environment

        1. There is no audience with which to communicate

        2. The microphone is the extension of the performer

        3. The performance is stored on tape

    C. Some musicians are not suited to both live and studio situations

    D. Some performers blend both experiences

        1. Have portions of prerecorded music to which they play or sing

        2. Some performers LIP SYNC an entire performance, i.e., they mouth the words to a prerecorded performance

    E. There has been a gradual transition from live performances to recorded performances in the last fifty years

II. New Concepts in Notation and the Lack of It (pp. 310-313)

    A. Studio recording involves both concert and commercial music

    B. Classical concert music is often recorded during a performance

        1. In front of an audience

        2. Musicians read traditional notated music

        3. Composer is rarely involved

        4. The studio is rarely used to "work out ideas"

    C. Commercial music is often composed in the studio

        1. Music is rarely in traditional notation

        2. Groups rehearse with the composer, create final product through COLLECTIVE COMPOSITION

            a. Musicians work together to finish a composition

            b. Performers play musical ideas specific to their instruments

            c. Rhythm sections are most often involved in this process

        3. Studio often serves as an environment for composition and performance

D. Recording film scores

   1. Through the early 1970s, this reflected the notational tradition of classical music

      a. Musicians played whatever was placed in front of them

      b. Musicians were hired for their reading skills rather than improvisational skills

   2. The rhythm section improvised musical ideas based on shorthand notations

E. HENRY MANCINI (see biography, pp. 311-312) exemplifies the diverse abilities of studio composers

   1. Composes both original and imitative music

   2. Can write music that imitates almost any style

   3. Film and television composers must be able to produce unobtrusive music quickly

F. The recording studio is a controlled environment

   1. Instruments that are difficult to hear in a live performance can be heard easily

   2. The balance between instruments is determined by the audio engineer in the MIX

      a. The process of blending instruments together into a musical whole

      b. Performed electronically by the engineers

      c. Control of the sound is in the hands of engineers rather than the musicians

      d. Soft sounding instruments can compete easily with louder instruments

   3. Mancini was one of the first to take advantage of the possibilities of studio manipulation

      a. New instrumental combinations are possible

      b. Mancini has produced some of the most popular sounds in commercial music

G. LISTENING NOTES: *A Cool Shade of Blue* (pp. 312-313)

   1. Uses exotic instruments and performance techniques

   2. Uses many electronic studio EFFECTS

      a. Electronically alters the sound of an instrument

      b. Also called SIGNAL PROCESSING

      c. REVERB (REVERBERATION)

         i. An echo effect

         ii. Originally from the natural echo of the room in which the recording took place

         iii. Now produced by digital sound processors

      d. Other electronic effects include ECHO and CHORUS

   3. Style of this piece is based on THIRD STREAM jazz and COOL or WEST COAST jazz

      a. Third stream jazz

         i. Uses elements of classical music

         ii. Combined with elements of jazz

      b. Cool jazz or West Coast jazz

         i. Post bebop style of jazz

       ii.   Softened some of the aggressive elements of bebop

       iii. Melodies in a comfortable range

       iv. Fewer explosive sounds in the rhythm section

       v.   Tempos were more relaxed than in bebop

  c. This music is typical of movie soundtracks in the 1960s

III. The Studio Musician: Multitrack Recordings (p. 313)

  A. Composing, rehearsing, and recording music has changed dramatically in the last thirty years

  B. MULTITRACK recording techniques have been developed in the studio

    1. Musicians no longer have to record at the same time

    2. Individual parts or TRACKS are recorded separately and mixed later

    3. The music is LAYERED from the fundamental rhythm tracks to the main melody

    4. Musicians record their parts against previoulsly recorded tracks

  C. The communication between musicians has been changed a great deal

    1. First musicians to record must be aware of what will be recorded later

    2. Later performers must respond to what is already recorded

    3. Later performers cannot obviously influence what has already been recorded

IV. Production Techniques (pp. 313-316)

  A. The producer guides and coordinates the composer, musicians, and engineers to create the final project

  B. QUINCY JONES (see biography, pp. 314-315)

    1. Has been involved for several years as a composer, performer, and producer

    2. He is one of the most successful producers in history

      a. He has a thorough knowledge of the music market

      b. Also has a thorough knowledge of all aspects of production

    3. Combines his traditional musical background with his composing and performing skills

    4. Is well known as an improvisor, performer, and composer as well as producer

    5. He uses his knowledge of the current music market to create unique works

    6. He has used his production skils for a wide variety of performers

      a. James Ingram

      b. George Benson

      c. The Pointer Sisters

      d. Michael Jackson

    7. LISTENING NOTES: "The Places You Find Love" from *Back on the Block* (pp. 315-316)

V. Music Videos

  A. The studio has grown in concept alongside the development of the music video

  B. Many early video productions were films of live performances

C. Video soon expanded to become an interpretation of the text

    1. Carrying on the tradition of word painting

    2. With recent technological advances, videos have become huge productions

D. Competition in the commercial market has intensified dramatically

    1. The cost of recording one song or video can exceed thousands of dollars

    2. The chance for new talent to find exposure has diminished greatly because of costs

    3. The number of people required to produce a a recording and video is huge

    4. The days of one artist controlling all the aspects of a commercial production are gone

EXERCISES

1 Choose one of your all-time favorite films to study the soundtrack. Make note of who the composer is and who the music editor is (usually two different people). Watch the film several times, playing and replaying important scenes. Take note of how the music is used in these important scenes. For example, how is the music performed in a chase sequence? In a romantic scene? A scary or suspenseful scene? What kinds of instruments are used for specific situations? In the film you have chosen, is the music effective or overpowering or comical? What amount of the music is pre-recorded (hit songs, jazz standards, folk songs, etc.) and how are these used in the film? Do they help establish a time period or a character's personality? What amount of the music was composed specifically for that film? How effective is the newly composed music? Do you feel that the music soundtrack influenced your original opinion of this film? After studying the soundtrack extensively, has your opinion of this film increased or decreased?

2. Watch one hour of MTV or VH-1 or some other music video television per day for one week. You do not necessarily need to watch for one straight hour, and in fact it may be more entertaining to watch ten minutes at one time of day and thirty minutes at a later time. Keep a log of the videos that are played, including such information as group, title of song, title of album, style of music (such as rap, grunge, speed metal, oldie, whatever). Also make notes in your log on your personal opinions of the various videos you see. Which are good songs, which are bad, which are more effective with video, and which sound better on the radio with no video. Try to watch a variety of styles rather than keeping track of the same style, partly to expose yourself to other songs and partly because with the same style (such as "Headbanger's Ball" or "MTV Raps") you are more likely to see the same videos several times in one week. As a sideline, you may want to take note of the commercials that are played between videos. Do they imitate the music videos you have been watching? Are they imitative in musical style or video content, or both? Are they aimed at a specific audience that may be watching a specific style of video?

STUDY QUESTIONS

1. The common environment for composers and performers in most contemporary styles is (p. 309)

   A.   The concert hall

   B   The recording studio

   C.   The radio station

   D.   The television station

2. Besides performing to an audience, performers must also play to _____. (p. 309)

3. The pressure for a perfect performance is less in a live situation than in a recording situation. (p. 309)

   A.   True

   B.   False

4. Studio musicians perform in an isolated environment because (p. 309)

   A.   There is no audience with which to communicate

   B.   Most studios have soundproof booths to keep out background noise

   C.   The lighting is kept very low in most recording studios

   D.   Most recording sessions take place very late at night or very early in the morning

5. In recording classical concert music, the composer is rarely involved with the recording. (p. 310)

   A.   True

   B.   False

6. The process in which the musicians work out ideas specific to their instruments to create the final product is called _____ _____. (p. 310)

7. The musicians who are most commonly involved with this process are (p. 310)

   A.   The horn section

   B.   The lead guitars

   C.   The rhythm section

   D.   The lead and backing vocalists

8. The studio is an environment for _____ and _____. (p. 310)

9. Classical music often uses the studio to work out new ideas. (p. 310)

   A.   True

   B.   False

10. Through the early 1970s, the process of recording film scores reflected the _____ tradition of classical music. (p. 310)

   A.   Improvisational

   B.   Notational

   C.   Atonal

   D.   Chromatic

11. Musicians were hired for film scores primarily for their (p. 310)

    A.   Improvisational skills

    B.   Instrumental range

    C.   Ability to blend their sound

    D.   Reading skills

12. Composers for _____ and _____ are required to produce chameleonlike sounds quickly and accurately. (p. 310)

13. In a recording studio, instruments are recorded separately and then blended into the final product through the process of _____. (p. 310)

14. In the recording studio, the above named process is performed electronically by (p. 310)

    A.   The producer

    B.   The production coordinator

    C.   The audio engineer

    D.   The mixmaster

15. Because the studio is a controlled environment, all instruments can be heard equally. (p. 310)

    A.   True

    B.   False

16. In the studio, control of the sound is in the hands of (p. 310)

    A.   Engineers

    B.   Vocalists

    C.   Instrumentalists

    D.   Producers

17. One of the first composers to take full advantage of new instrumental combinations available through studio manipulation was (p. 310)

    A.   Quincy Jones

    B.   Duke Ellington

    C.   Henry Mancini

    D.   Dmitri Tiomkin

18. An echo effect that is taken from the sound of the room in which the recording is made is called _____. (p. 312)

19. The process of changing the original sound of an instrument is _____. (p. 312)

20. Enhancing the natural acoustic sound of an instrument with electronic gadgetry such as echo or delay is called _____ processing. (p. 312)

21. Using electronic effects can be seen as an extension of using mutes. (p. 312)

    A.   True

    B.   False

22. The jazz style that incorporates elements from classical music is called (p. 312)

    A.   Dixieland

    B.   Third stream

    C.   Hard bop

    D.   Cool jazz

23. The jazz style that softened the aggressive elements of bebop is called (p. 312)

    A.   Dixieland

    B.   Third stream

    C.   Hard bop

    D.   Cool jazz

24. The above named jazz style is also referred to as _____ _____ jazz. (p. 312)

25. Which of the following is NOT a characteristic of the jazz style named in question 23? (p. 312)

    A.   The melody is played in a comfortable range

    B.   The tempos are relaxed and a bit slower

    C.   Serial composition technique may be used

    D.   The rhythm section is less explosive sounding

26. The recording technique in which each musician records his or her part individually so that the engineer can mix them later is called _____ recording. (p. 313)

27. Each individual recorded part is called a (p. 313)

    A.   Track

    B.   Fragment

    C.   Segment

    D.   Motive

28. In the recording style named in question 26, the various sounds are layered onto the fundamental _____ _____. (p. 313)

29. The person who coordinates the composer, musicians, and engineers is the _____. (p. 313)

30. The knowledge of what two elements of the music business has made Quincy Jones one of the most successful producers in history? (pp. 313-314)

    A.   _____

    B.   _____

31. As an improvisor, composer, and performer, Megill has compared Quincy Jones to which three classical composers? (p. 314)

    A.   _____

    B.   _____

    C.   _____

32. Quincy Jones has not composed film soundtracks. (p. 315)

    A. True

    B. False

33. What medium is the extension of the sound recording? (p. 316)

    _____

34. The interpretation of lyrics in a music video is an extension of what compositional device? (p. 316)

    _____

35. The chance for new performers to find exposure for their product has diminished because of (p. 317)

    A. The lack of genuine musical talent

    B. The high cost of producing an audio or video recording

    C. The lack of knowledge of computer technology

    D. The snobbery of MTV and VH-1

36. The days of one artist controlling all aspects of a commercial production are gone. (p. 317)

    A. True

    B. False

ANSWER KEY

CHAPTER 1

1. C

2. Overtone series

3. False

4. D

5. B

6. False

7. D

8. Intonation

9. Sampling

10. True

11. Industrial

CHAPTER 2

1. Strings, woodwinds, brass, and percussion

2. A

3. True

4. Low or long

5. Drawing a bow across the strings

6. C

7. B

8. Percussive

9. A

10. Single

11. Double

12. False

13. B

14. False

15. Opening more tubing

16. Slide

17. False

18. Struck or hit

19. True

20. D

21. Because they blend well together

22. B

23. True

24. Viol

25. Harpsichord

26. Pairs

27. C

28. Clarinet, trumpet (or cornet), and trombone

29. B

30. D

31. Piano, guitar, bass, and drums

32. C

33. True

34. Musical Instrument Digital Interface

35. Sequencing

36. False

37. True

38. False

CHAPTER 3

1. Musical space

2. B

3. D

4. Simultaneous activity

5. C

6. The way in which beats are grouped together

7. True

8. False

9. Range

10. Attack, decay, sustain, and release

11. B

12. Melody

13. Conjunct

14. Disjunct

15. Articulation

16. A

17. True

18. C

19. Orchestration

20. B

21. D

22. True

23. Texture

24. Piano

25. Forte

26. Fortissimo

27. True

28. False

29. A metronome

30. B

31. A

32. Chord

33. False

34. Tension

35. Harmonic rhythm

36. True

37. Texture

38. A

39. C

40. B

41. If new sounds are discovered; because of a growing need to communicate musical ideas

42. Raises

43. Lowers

44. C

45. D

46. A

47. Scales

48. Mode

49. Major and minor

50. B

51. Tonality or key

52. False

53. B

54. D

55. True

56. Cadence

57. C

58. Chromatic

59. Atonal

CHAPTER 4

1. To allow for diversity in sound; to give a feeling of unity to a work

2. B

3. Repetition, contrast

4. A B A

5. A B

6. C

7. Movements

8. True

9. A

10. D.

11. False

12. Transitional

13. To allow the work to unwind and come to a rest

14. True

15. True

16. A B A C A D A or A B A C A B A

17. False

18. C

19. Exposition

20. To break down themes into smaller units and to change keys

21. Modulation

22. False

23. Coda

24. Triple

25. Ternary

26. Binary

27. Scherzo

28. Counterpoint

29. B

30. Ostinato, Ground bass, or Basso ostinato

31. False

32. True

33. The subject

34. The answer

35. The countersubject

36. B

37. Music supplies rhythmic accents and flowing melodies that suggest movement

38. False

39. Musical theater

40. True

41. Dance and stagecraft

CHAPTER 5

1. C

2. True

3. Song and chant

4. Oral

5. Aboriginal

6. Because there were no notational systems

7. Pictures, wall sketches, statues, urns, writings

8. Because most secular music was not written down and has been lost

9. B

10. D

11. Byzantine and Ambrosian

12. It represents a concern for melodic construction; it supplied musical material for other compositions for hundreds of years

13. B

14. False

15. Modes, church modes, or scales

16. A

17. Because chant has never really left our culture

18. False

19. Boys singing a melody an octave higher than men

20. Organum

21. B

22. When the two voice parts moved in opposite directions as well as in parallel directions

23. C

24. Cantus firmus

25. The tenor

26. True

27. Minimize the contrast between parts and make the relationship between parts nearly equal

28. Notre Dame

29. C

30. Leonin and Perotin

31. Trinity

32. D

33. True

34. Motet

35. B

36. Ordinary

37. Proper

38. C

39. Notre Dame; Machaut

CHAPTER 6

1. B

2. False

3. Points of imitation

4. Cadence points

5. C

6. D

7. False

8. Imitation and polyphony

9. A cappella

10. A

11. C

12. To have a large range of notes; to parallel the vocal ranges in a choir

13. False

14. Cantus firmus

15. D

16. B

17. Madrigal

18. D

19. To musically stress a specific word; to make a word stand out from the other words around it

20. Madrigalisms

21. C

22. Homophonic verses; polyphonic refrains

23. C

24. D

25. A

26. B

27. Doubling

28. C

29. St. Mark's cathedral

30. Polychoral

31. Two choir lofts in St. Mark's cathedral

32. False

33. B

34. Baroque

CHAPTER 7

1. True

2. Emotion; Contrast

3. B

4. Florentine Camerata

5. A

6. Figured bass

7. Basso continuo

8. B

9. Ground bass

10. False

11. Opera

12. C

13. Sinfonias

14. To add contrast to the vocal sections

15. A

16. B

17. Virtuoso

18. D

19. Da capo

20. C

21. Dry

22. D

23. Castrati

24. To provide contrast and drama to the opera

25. Aria

26. Aria

27. Recitative

28. Aria

29. Recitative

30. Aria

31. Aria

32. Recitative

33. Aria

34. Recitative

35. Ballad

36. A

37. C

38. Oratorio

39. False

40. B

41. True

42. To express noble and sacred feelings

43. True

44. False

45. Cantata

46. A

47. Passion

48. True

49. False

50. C

51. C

52. Cello

53. Four

54. True

55. Suite

56. False

57. Dance steps

58. Orchestras, chamber ensembles, solo instruments, solo harpsichord

59. Concerto gross

60. Tutti; Ritornello

61. D

62. B

63. Terraced dynamics

64. Stops

65. C

66. Da camera

67. Da chiesa

68. True

69. D

70. Prelude; Toccata

71. Subject

72. C

73. B

74. Episodes

75. Chorale prelude

76. True

77. A

78. Jean-Philippe Rameau

79. Instrumental dances for ballet

CHAPTER 8

1. C

2. Galant

3. Reaction against the complex polyphony of the Baroque and a move to thin the texture

4. True

5. Vienna, Austria

6. Artists were obsessed with the cultural examples of ancient Greece and Rome, resulting in a classical attitude toward cultural expression

7. D

8. B

9. Motivic development

10. Instrumental suites; Sonatas

11. C

12. A

13. Minuet and trio

14. Sonata allegro

15. Exposition; Development; Recapitulation

16. C

17. A

18. Modulation

19. Both themes or theme groups remain in the tonic key

20. Rondo

21. B

22. Haydn

23. Esterhazy

24. Key area

25. D

26. B

27. Transitional

28. Motivic interplay; Modulation

29. Because of his increasing deafness

30. Publishing; Conducting; Yearly pensions from wealthy patrons

31. True

32. Soloist

33. False

34. C

35. False

36. D

37. A

38. Masses; Oratorios

39. B

40. True

41. Established the overture as an integral part of the opera; Used the orchestra thematically; Moved to more simple melodies and textures; Softened the contrast between arias and recitatives

42. Libretto

43. Opéra comique

44. Singspiel

45. Opera buffa

46. D

47. Ensemble finales

48. False

49. By controlling key areas; By manipulating thematic material

50. False

51. Patronage

52. Performing; Conducting; Publishing; Producing public concerts

53. A

54. D

55. C

CHAPTER 9

1. B

2. An art song

3. Lied

4. True

5. False

6. Word painting

7. Song cycle

8. C

9. D.

10. Strophic; Through-composed

11. Strophic

12. Contrast; Development

13. A

14. Modified strophic

15. False

16. Miniatures

17. Character

18. C

19. A

20. D

21. B

22. Chopin

23. Rubato

24. D

25. A

26. Concert overtures; Tone (or Symphonic) poems; Program symphonies

27. B.

28. Sonata-allegro; Rondo (or Irregular)

29. D

30. False

31. Idée fixe

32. True

33. Thematic transformation

34. The returning theme (idée fixe); The autobiographical program; The enlarged orchestra; Unusual orchestrations

35. It expanded the dynamic range

36. True

37. Orchestration

38. False

39. Emotion; Passion

40. Emotions are expanded; Magic; Supernatural suspense; Heroes and villains who are larger than life

41. Passionate

42. B

43. A

44. True

45. His ability to build strong musical characterizations

46. Music dramas

47. He felt they blended all aspects of music and drama

48. Myths; Legends

49. False

50. True

51. False

52. C

53. So there would be no interruption of the musical flow

54. Four

55. B

56. Motives

57. Leitmotivs

58. Developed; Transformed

59. To express the changing conditions of the plot and characters

60. True

61. False

62. To sing over the large orchestra

63. Nationalism

64. National identity

65. Use folk songs; Use folk dance rhythms; Use patriotic stories for opera plots

66. Italy; France; Germany

67. C

68. A

69. D

70. *Boris Godunov*

CHAPTER 10

1. Dissonance

2. A

3. C

4. Debussy

5. Fourths; Fifths

6. Resolution

7. D

8. Symbolism

9. Use of Eastern scales; Use of whole tone scales; use of chords built of fourths and fifths

10. C

11. Mallarmé

12. First

13. *Petrushka*

14. B

15. Pounding, irregular rhythms; Sharp dissonances; Unique orchestral colors

16. False

17. True

18. Philosophy; Technique

19. Overly emotional music of the late 19th century

20. Harmonies (dissonances); Forms (styles)

21. Restraint; Control

22. Musicology

23. Ethnomusicology

24. B

25. True

26. Folk music

27. A

28. False

29. Frustration, guilt, or terror

30. Atonality

31. D

32. D

33. Twelve-tone technique; Dodecaphony

34. False

35. Equality

36. Series; Tone row

37. B

38. Retrograde

39. Inversion

40. Transposition

41. C

42. Half-sung and half-spoken

43. Tone cluster

44. Henry Cowell; Charles Ives

45. With the palm of the hand; With the forearm; With the fist; With a short board

46. False

47. False

48. The use of polyrhythms; The idea of communal singing

49. Polyrhythms

50. Call-response

51. African rhythms and melodies; European harmonies

52. Call-response; Chord progressions

53. True

54. Third; Seventh

55. City; Country

56. B

57. A

58. C

59. D

60 An ostinato

61. A riff

62. A

63. Collective improvisation

64. False

65. True

66. Swing

67. A layback

68. True

69. To maintain a constant pulse; To add color through the use of cymbals, bells, etc.

70. To generate a metric pulse; To supply the fundamental harmonic progression

71. Comping

72. B

73. Technical virtuosity; Angular compositions

74. Charlie Parker; Dizzy Gillespie

75. Walking

76. Bombs (dropping bombs)

CHAPTER 11

1. True

2. Pitch

3. A

4. Karlheinz Stockhausen

5. False

6. B

7. True

8. C

9. Artificial intelligence

10. C

11. Prepared

12. True

13. B

14. A

15. True

16. Tape manipulation

17. Musique concrète

18. C

19. Synthesizers

20. False

21. C

22. B

23. Speech and theater

24. True

25. For the musician to play as much as possible

26. C

27. Traditional concepts

28. True

29. To have a single event last for a large period of time

30. True

31. Eastern ideals, philosophies, or religions

32. African drumming

33. False

34. D

35. False

36. Neoromantic

37. A

38. True

39. C

40. B

41. Classical

42. Serial technique; Traditional orchestral instruments; Classical forms; Improvisation

43. C

44. Atonality

45. True

46. One is played by jazz musicians and the other is played by classical musicians

47. D

48. C

49. False

50. True

51. Crossover

CHAPTER 12

1. True

2. C

3. Blues; Work songs; Rags; Gospel; Rhythm & blues; Country western

4. Tin Pan Alley

5. False

6. False

7. Rhythm & blues; Country

8. Country blues

9. Rhythm & blues

10. Amplification (amplified sound)

11. Tenor saxophone

12. False

13. True

14. B

15. False

16. False

17. True

18. The Beatles

19. Classical concepts; New recording techniques; Jazz ideas; Experimental sounds

20. D

21. A

22. *Sgt. Pepper's Lonely Hearts Club Band*

23. Cultural backgrounds

24. Good times; Security

25. Rebellion; The need for change

26. Soul

27. Detroit

28. Motown

29. True

30. The electric guitar

31. Jimi Hendrix

32. Feedback (distortion)

33. B

34. D

35. Realistic

36. Storage; Synthesis; Processing

37. A

38. A heavy bass drum on each beat of each measure

39. Punk

40. Fusion (jazz-rock fusion)

41. C

42. Producing

43. C

44. High volume levels; Thick electronic texture

45. True

46. Rebellious

47. Experimental rock

48. Caustic; Angry

49. Rap

50. Black identity

51. B

52. Harmonic; Rhythmic and metric

53. True

54. Music video

55. True

56. They do not perform live concerts, they only produce recordings and videos

57. False

TOPIC 1

1. B

2. D

3. Scoring

4. True

5. Themes; Melodies

6. A

7. Improvisation

8. False

9. B

10. True

11. C

12. B

13. True

14. D

15. Compositional

16. A

17. True

18. C

19. False

20. False

21. B

22. C

23. A hymn

24. A

25. C

26. Essercizi (Exercises)

27. D

28. Tone poem

29. B

30. False

31. True

32. Jazz; Experimental classical

33. When the music is not specifically notated

34. Standards

35. C

36. A

37. Harmonic extensions

38. B

39. Ornamentation

40. Interpretation

41. False

TOPIC 2

1. Solo instruments; Combinations

2. B

3. C

4. Trombone; Piccolo; Contrabassoon

5. Choir

6. False

7. A

8. True

9. The use of new instruments; The use of new combinations of traditional instruments

10. True

11. Valves

12. False

13. The four movement structure

14. Movement

15. False

16. C

17. B

18. D

19. Organic

20. A scherzo

21. B

22. True

23. A

24. True

25. Orchestra

26. C

27. False

28. B

29. New York Philharmonic Society; Metropolitan Opera House

30. Instrumentation; Structure

31. False

32. True

33. Contrapuntal writing

34. True

35. Chamber music

36. D

37. His ability to control a vast orchestra

38. Expanded

TOPIC 3

1. True

2. C

3. B

4. Emphasize

5. A cantus firmus

6. Tenor

7. True

8. False

9. Focusing on the music rather than on the words

10. A

11. Chanson

12. Word painting

13. D

14. A

15. False

16. B

17. Monody

18. True

19. D

20. Poets; Composers

21. False

22. The interpretation of words in general and painting specific words

23. Sprechstimme

24. C

25. Subject matter

26. A

27. True

28. B

29. Rhythmic

30. True

31. D

32. Low

33. A

34. False

35. C

36. D

37. C

38. A

39. Nostalgic

40. Development

41. True

42. C

43. A symphony

44. Variations

45. Tonality

46. Orchestral

47. False

48. B

49. Verbal polyglot

50. D

51. False

52. True

TOPIC 4

1. True

2. C

3. Terraced dynamics

4. False

5. A

6. Crescendo

7. Decrescendo

8. B

9. C

10. Taktus

11. True

12. D

13. True

14. B

15. Concert master

16. A

17. C

18. D

19. B

20. Baton (stick)

21. False

22. Interpretation

23. B

24. True

25. Melody; Tempo

26. C

27. Expression

28. A

29. True

30. Stylistically

31. False

32. In order to communicate effectively with the players and use rehearsal time effectively

33. Because there is a vast number of works available to study and perform

34. Visual representation

35. C

36. True

37. Conductor; Performer; Audience

38. B

39. False

40. A

41. True

42. Symphonic

43. Excerpt

44. C

45. Interpretation

46. True

47. B

48. True

TOPIC 5

1. C
2. B
3. Corelli; Vivaldi
4. True
5. Concerto grosso
6. C
7. D
8. False
9. True
10. A cadenza
11. B
12. A
13. B
14. Sonata-allegro
15. Slow
16. C
17. Piano
18. Trumpet
19. Haydn; Mozart
20. Orchestra
21. C
22. A
23. False
24. D
25. False
26. B
27. Different combinations
28. D
29. B
30. Harpsichord
31. A
32. C
33. Concertino group
34. Concerto
35. Sonata

36. B

37. Violin

38. A

39. D

40. Three

41. A continuo

42. B

43. Because they can supply their own accompaniment

44. Multimovement keyboard suite

45. Construction

46. True

47. The ending is expanded to include an additional development section and a second coda

TOPIC 6

1. Intimate

2. C

3. B

4. True

5. D

6. Divertimenti

7. C

8. False

9. True

10. Homophonic

11. Melodic lines

12. Developmental writing

13. A

14. C

15. B

16. D

17. A

18. True

19. Introspective

20. Fugal (Fugue)

21. Aggressive virtuosity

22. Dissonance; Rhythmic complexity

23. B

24. D

25. Tonality; Sonata form

26. C

27. A

28. D

29. Atonality

30. Regular metric; Angular

31. Rhythmic

32. Because of their subtlety and refinement

33. C

34. B

35. Walking

36. True

37. A

38. False

TOPIC 7

1. False

2. Europe; Africa

3. Blues; Gospel; Jazz

4. C

5. A

6. True

7. B

8. Several activities occurring simultaneously

9. True

10. A

11. D

12. Polytonality

13. B

14. Because it is supposed to be performed by all humanity on every hill and dale

15. Classical; Jazz; Commercial

16. *Rhapsody In Blue*

17. C

18. False

19. True

20. D

21. Syncopations

22. Unique musical style; The subject matter

23. True

24. Dissonant; Powerful; Concise

25. B

26. Folklore

27 *Billy the Kid*; *Rodeo*; *Appalachian Spring*

28. False

29. Percussive; Syncopated

30. A

31. Glissando

32. Jazz

33. False

34. An improvisatory

35. C

36. Composer/arranger; Pianist; Band leader

37. A

38. False

39. True

40. B

41. False

42. Harmonic

43. D

44. Colleges and universities; Film production; Musical theater; Jazz bands; Commercial music performances; Rock music performances; At home

TOPIC 8

1. C

2. Global unity

3. A

4. Ethnomusicology

5. Tradition; Culture

6. B

7. True

8. Familiarity; Exposure

9. Tradition

10. True

11. Movie soundtracks

12. False

13. Audio; Video

14. B

15. D

16. Heritage; Ethnic identity

17. C

18. True

19. History; Society rules; Morals

20. A

21. True

22. D

23. True

24. B

25. B

26. C

27. D

28. A

29. Tritonic

30. Microtonal

31. D

32. B

33. D

34. Polyrhythms

35. Africa; India; Latin America

36. Modulated

37. False

38. True

39. Drone

40. C

41. C

42. Microtonal

43. Tabla; Baya

44. B

45. A

46. D

47. False

48. Pentatonic

49. B

50. True

51. A

52. C

53. Pentatonic

54. B

55. Breathy

56. Three

57. C

58. False

59. Nasal

60. D

TOPIC 9

1. True

2. Film

3. B

4. True

5. False

6. Multimedia

7. C

8. False

9. Minstrel shows; Burlesque; Vaudeville

10. Musical events

11. Musical comedy

12. D

13. B

14. Jerome Kern; Oscar Hammerstein II

15. A

16. C

17. Cole Porter; Irving Berlin

18. B

19. Controversial; Political

20. C

21. By having plots dominated by stories about singers and dancers who then had a good excuse to break into a musical number. A "show within a show."

22. D

23. Themes; Motives

24. A

25. Clarity of words

26. D

27. B

28. True

29. C

30. A

31. B

32. D

33. Ballad opera

34. False

35. Andrew Lloyd Webber

36. B

37. True

38. Music that never stops (a continuous flow of music)

39. Emotional development

40. C

41. False

42. Ensemble finale

43. Several characters sing simultaneously; They sing separate and overlapping lines; Each character expresses a different emotion; Each character sings a different text

44. Contemporary rock music

TOPIC 10

1. B

2. Microphones

3. True

4. A

5. True

6. Collective composition

7. C

8. Composition; Performance

9. False

10. B

11. D

12. Film; Television

13. Mixing

14. C

15. True

16. A

17. C

18. Reverb

19. An effect

20. Signal

21. True

22. B

23. D

24. West Coast

25. C

26. Multitrack

27. A

28. Rhythm track

29. Producer

30. The music market; All aspects of record production

31. Mozart; Beethoven; Wagner

32. False

33. Music video

34. Word painting

35. B

36. True